Pocket GCSE Greek Etymological Lexicon

ALSO AVAILABLE FROM BLOOMSBURY

Pocket GCSE Latin Etymological Lexicon by Caroline K. Mackenzie

Greek to GCSE Part 1 by John Taylor

Greek to GCSE Part 2 by John Taylor

OCR Anthology for Classical Greek GCSE 2027–2028
by Christopher Burnand and Andy Mylne

Greek Stories by John Taylor and Kristian Waite

Pocket GCSE Greek Etymological Lexicon

Caroline K. Mackenzie

BLOOMSBURY ACADEMIC
LONDON • NEW YORK • OXFORD • NEW DELHI • SYDNEY

BLOOMSBURY ACADEMIC
Bloomsbury Publishing Plc, 50 Bedford Square, London, WC1B 3DP, UK
Bloomsbury Publishing Inc, 1359 Broadway, New York, NY 10018, USA
Bloomsbury Publishing Ireland, 29 Earlsfort Terrace, Dublin 2, D02 AY28, Ireland

BLOOMSBURY, BLOOMSBURY ACADEMIC and the Diana logo are trademarks of Bloomsbury Publishing Plc

First published in Great Britain 2026

Cover image: Women carding wool depicted in the Attic red-figure drinking cup by the Douris Painter *c.* 480–470 BC found in Vulci, Italy. Azoor Photo/Alamy Stock Photo

A catalogue record for this book is available from the British Library.

A catalog record for this book is available from the Library of Congress.

ISBN: PB: 978-1-3505-7211-9
ePDF: 978-1-3505-7213-3
eBook: 978-1-3505-7212-6

Typeset by RefineCatch Limited, Bungay, Suffolk
Printed and bound in Great Britain

For product safety related questions contact productsafety@bloomsbury.com.

To find out more about our authors and books visit www.bloomsbury.com and sign up for our newsletters.

For my parents, with love.

Contents

Acknowledgements

Thank you to Alice Wright for commissioning this lexicon and for her support and encouragement. With thanks also to Lucy Batrouney, Lucy Springett and Sophie Beardsworth for skilfully steering it home, and to all the team at Classical Studies, Bloomsbury. Many thanks to Merv Honeywood and his team at RefineCatch Limited. Thank you to Brenna Akerman and Sarah Ruddock for their enthusiasm and for including me in many varied and interesting Bloomsbury Classics projects.

Huge thanks, Barbarann, for your lovely illustrations and for your passion for the project. It was such a delight to collaborate on this and to see your fabulous artwork evolve, inspired by the Greek words. Thank you also, Frank, for your support and input.

My Classics journey began at school with a wonderful teacher, Mrs Ruscoe, who loved Greek even more than Latin. On retirement she and her husband moved to Greece where they had spent all the school holidays. Although Mrs Ruscoe is sadly no longer with us, I hope she would have enjoyed this little lexicon. While at school, I was also fortunate to attend the JACT Greek summer school at Bryanston three times, where my love of ancient Greek was taken to new levels. James Morwood and

David Raeburn (particularly his Greek plays, performed in the original) were part of the joy of Bryanston. In a lovely ring composition, they offered renewed encouragement through hand-written letters and nostalgic conversations when I embarked on my Classics career after an odyssey into the law.

John Taylor was an ally and a muse when we were teaching in nearby schools. A highlight was attending a Classics study day organised by John with my Year 8, who were more excited about meeting John than the character dressed up as a Roman soldier, who was pretty stiff competition. Thank you, John, for your continued support and for always happily answering my random questions on all things Greek (and Latin).

A special thank you to all my tutees, past and present, from ages eight to eighty-eight. Whether in one-to-one lessons, or group classes, your dedication and delight in learning Classics make my work so enriching. διδάσκω τε καί μανθάνω.

Classics Club started as an excuse to share a love of the Classical world with coffee and cake. Six years on, it has grown into a close-knit family, the members having shared so much together. I cannot thank each of you enough for the joy you bring to Mondays, and all the days in-between. You do not fail to impress me with your commitment, cheerfulness, and plethora of talents. A special shout-out to Kevin whose recitals of Greek dactylic hexameters, iambic trimeters and anapaests have become legendary.

Thank you, Allan, for over ten rewarding years of Greek together and for all your support.

Thank you, Kevin and Allan, for kindly reading a draft of the lexicon and for your insightful comments and numerous, excellent suggestions. Professor Armand D'Angour kindly advised on the footnotes relating to ancient Greek music, for which I am very grateful. Thank you also to the two anonymous peer reviewers for providing their expertise and for their very helpful and thoughtful notes. Any errors which remain are, of course, my own.

The very first derivative in this lexicon is thanks to Sophie Barker: during a Greek lesson (just before submission of my manuscript) I asked Sophie to suggest a way of remembering 'ἀγαθός' and, after careful thought, she replied that she thought *Agatha* Christie's books were really *good.*

Professor Richard Hunter kindly took me on as an eighteen-year-old undergraduate and directed my studies for three very happy years at Pembroke. Richard also supported me (both on paper and in person over a coffee in Cambridge) when I decided, a mere twenty years after graduating, finally to pursue postgraduate studies in Classics. Returning 'home' after twenty years away was serendipitously similar to my favourite Greek story, Homer's *Odyssey.*

Most of all, thank you to my friends and family who have journeyed with me on my odyssey through life, especially: Caroline, Phil, Arthur, with a special mention for my godson, Benedict; Lucy, Brian and Sheenagh; Myra and Robin; Akiko; Ursula; Janet and Gordon (who has been a willing and knowledgeable companion at many Greek plays in London). For being such a glamorous, inspirational and supportive aunt and uncle (despite the transatlantic distance), thanks and love to Penny and Mike. For being a brilliant and kind sister and nephew, love to Liz and Tom: thank you for all the books, chocolate and memories. For absolutely everything, heartfelt thanks to Dad (whom we all miss so much) and Mum, to both of whom this lexicon is dedicated, with love. Thank you for giving me my first Greek lexicon – an intermediate Liddell and Scott – when I was sixteen. To my lovely brother, Jamie, for insisting on making a special book cover for it, knowing how much it would be used. It still has pride of place (in its home-made cover) on my bookshelves.Thank you, Dad, for cutting out and saving for me Classics-related articles in the newspapers in the days before the internet; and Mum, for still doing so. Thank you both for being such lovely parents to us all. For Grannie, whose unique blend of kindness and mischief is unmatched. Last but not least: to my husband, Jock, the words for whom I leave to Homer.

'…οὐ μὲν γὰρ τοῦ γε κρεῖσσον καὶ ἄρειον,
ἢ ὅθ᾽ ὁμοφρονέοντε νοήμασιν οἶκον ἔχητον'

Odyssey 6.182-3.

Introduction

There are many excellent reasons to learn ancient Greek, not least to be able to read Homer, the playwrights and other poets/ authors in the original. Students of the language may say that the joy of translating Greek is sufficient reward on its own. The skills acquired in learning to translate Greek are appreciated by logophiles, who may be learning ancient Greek alongside modern languages, and also by mathematicians who equate the logic and puzzle-solving qualities of translating with algebra. The letter 'π' has an important role in school Maths lessons and indeed has its own place on a calculator. Students of medicine who know some Greek will instantly recognise the meanings of many medical terms; they will also use the Greek letter 'μ' (mu) to indicate 'microgram', or 'μg', in their prescriptions. 'μg' also appears on cereal packets and vitamin bottles.

During the recent pandemic – see 'πᾶς' and 'δῆμος' (literally, affecting 'a whole people') – the Greek alphabet was used by the World Heath Organisation ('WHO') to label key variants of the virus that causes COVID-19. WHO issued a press release explaining that it had 'assigned simple, easy to say and remember labels… using letters of the Greek alphabet' because 'scientific names can be difficult to say and recall, and are prone to misreporting.'[1]

For candidates working towards an examination in classical Greek, a knowledge of the links to English is usually a requirement. The language specification for the OCR GCSE Classical Greek qualification ('GCSE') states, 'Learners should be able to explain the derivation of English words from Classical Greek as evidence of the continuing influence of the classical world on later times.' The Intermediate Certificate in Classical Greek ('ICCG') specification states that one of the aims of the course is to encourage 'an awareness of the influence of Classical Greek on the languages of today.'

The aims of this lexicon are to help students not only learn vocabulary, but also to appreciate the ubiquity of Greek in the English language. Some of the derivatives may already be well-known (although perhaps not their exact Greek origin). The derivatives that are not familiar may help expand learners' English vocabulary, too. It is hoped learners will be encouraged to explore some of the unknown English words. Essentially, the lexicon can be used as a starting point for a discussion of derivatives. The extent to which the entries for each Greek word

---

[1] https://www.who.int/news/item/31-05-2021-who-announces-simple-easy-to-say-labels-for-sars-cov-2-variants-of-interest-and-concern.

are explored can be tailored to individual students' needs. A deep dive into derivatives could be a useful extension activity in the classroom and may also be a worthwhile pursuit in post-GCSE studies, whether in Classics or another discipline.

Derivatives in other disciplines

Greek derivatives give us the names of many subjects on the school curriculum, e.g. biology, geography, physics, mathematics, and Greek also accounts for many specialist terms within these subjects. While knowledge of specialist terms is certainly not assumed, a selection has been included (often with a footnote flagging the area of specialism) partly for those who wish to explore a particular topic further, and partly to demonstrate the ubiquity and usefulness of Greek in other subjects.

Greek's influence also extends beyond the school curriculum, to university subjects and careers. Again, the subject names often owe their origins to Greek, e.g. philosophy, architecture, botany, genetics, etc. and their specialist vocabularies are full of Greek derivatives. Some of these have been flagged in footnotes, for the same reasons as above. Many of the words in this lexicon are from the world of medicine and represent just an iota of the huge debt medical terminology owes to Greek. Other words in the lexicon relate to religion, nature, IT/computers, music, and even beauty treatments.

Greek language as a gateway, or 'πύλη', to the ancient Greek world

One of the joys of learning ancient Greek is that it unlocks a whole world of literature, art, history, culture, mythology, archaeology and philosophy. Indeed, one of the aims of the ICCG is 'to encourage candidates to develop an appreciation for Classical Greek history and culture, as exemplified in stories about Greek myth and history.'

Therefore, the footnotes in this lexicon often give further background or examples of highlights from the ancient Greek world. Some of them overlap with studies of Classical Civilisation and Ancient History. All of them are hoped to pique the interest of students who may be considering going on to study Classics at university. They include references to Greek theatre, statues, pottery, temples and music.

Greek and Latin

A knowledge of Latin is not assumed, nor needed, when reading this lexicon. There are some similarities between Greek and Latin words and a few of these are noted in the entries, where *The Chambers Dictionary* cites the etymology of a particular word as deriving from the Latin. Students of Latin may enjoy spotting 'double derivatives' where words are made up of a combination of a Greek root, as well as a Latin one, e.g. see 'agriscience'.

Differences between the GCSE and ICCG Defined Vocabulary Lists ('DVLs') – notation

The GCSE DVL contains 409 entries, all of which are included in this lexicon.

The ICCG DVL contains 250 entries: 234 of these words (marked in this lexicon with a single asterisk *) are on the GCSE DVL, the additional 16 words (marked in this lexicon with a double asterisk **) are not on the GCSE DVL.

Therefore, GCSE students need to know all the entries in this lexicon other than the 16 entries with a double asterisk **; ICCG students need to know all the entries which are asterisked (whether with one or two asterisks).

Differences between the GCSE and ICCG Defined Vocabulary Lists ('DVLs') – compound verbs

For GCSE, candidates are expected to work out the meanings of compound verbs where basic prepositions are used as prefixes, e.g. 'ἐκβάλλω' ('I throw out'). Therefore the entries in this lexicon (which reflect the GCSE DVL) do not include every example of such verbs. However, those compound verbs which are included on the ICCG DVL, e.g. 'ἐκβαίνω' ('I go out'), are included in this lexicon and, because they fall within those compound verbs which GCSE candidates are expected to work out, they are shown as needed for GCSE. In other words, this lexicon lists some (but not all) of the compound verbs needed for GCSE.

The order of words on the DVLs

The entries in the lexicon follow as far as possible the order of the GCSE DVL, with sub-entries immediately following their headword, e.g. 'ἐγώ' ('I') followed by 'ἐμός' ('my'). This means that occasionally the entries are not strictly alphabetical. However, it ensures, for the most part, consistency with the order of entries on the GCSE DVL. The words which are taken from the ICCG DVL alone have been inserted alphabetically.

Adjectives and adverbs

GCSE candidates are required to know the formation and declension of the comparatives and superlatives of adjectives and adverbs in the GCSE DVL. Such comparatives and superlatives are not given on the GCSE DVL and are therefore only included in this lexicon if they are specified on the ICCG DVL. A few additional examples have been included in the footnotes, e.g. the superlative of 'ἀγαθός' ('good') is 'ἄριστος' ('best', 'very good') which gives us words such as 'aristocracy'. This is an exercise which could be continued as an extension activity.

Nouns

The genitive stem of a noun is very important, as it provides the stem for all other cases, and should be learned with the nominative. English derivatives are often formed from it, e.g. 'παῖς, παιδός' ('child') gives us the prefix 'paed-' or 'paid-' as in 'paediatric', and 'πούς, ποδός' ('foot') gives us the suffix '-pod' as in 'decapod'.

Verbs

Where a Greek verb has a strong aorist, the aorist stem is often a clue to English derivatives, e.g. 'μανθάνω' ('I learn') has an aorist stem 'μαθ-' which gives us 'mathematics'. It is good practice to learn all parts of a verb given in a DVL together with its meaning.

Derivatives and their root words

Some of the derivatives in this lexicon may strictly originate from a Greek word which is not on the DVL but which has the same root as the word which is on the DVL. Rather than include too many additional Greek words which students do not need to learn for ICCG or GCSE, these derivatives are simply included under the word which is on the respective DVL. For example, the entry for 'ἡδύς, ἡδεῖα, ἡδύ' ('pleasant, sweet') includes derivatives such as 'hedonism', which is perhaps more closely related to the Greek word 'ἡδονή' ('pleasure'). Likewise, 'δοκεῖ (μοι), δόξει, ἔδοξε' ('(I) decide (= it seems good (to me))') includes derivatives such as 'orthodoxy' and 'paradox', which are perhaps more closely related to the Greek word 'δόξα' ('opinion'). However, it is hoped that these provide a useful connection to the words that need to be learned.

Cross-referencing

Where an entry is related to another word, e.g. a noun with the same root as a verb, the derivatives have not been repeated but the reader is directed to the main entry. For example, the entry for the noun 'φίλος, φίλου, ὁ' directs the reader to the verb 'φιλέω'. Usually the derivatives are included with the verb, but there are some exceptions where the connections may more easily be made with another form of the word.

'cf.' (an abbreviation from the Latin word 'confer' meaning 'compare') indicates that the reader should compare a corresponding entry, usually because the derivative is made up of more than one Greek word.

Some Greek words, e.g. 'γράφω' and 'λόγος' appear with such frequency in derivatives that these have not been cross-referenced every time. Students may wish to annotate these (and other cross-references which have been left for further discovery) whenever they spot them.

Privative alpha

In English, 'a-' or 'an-' is a prefix which signifies 'without', 'not' or 'opposite to'. It derives from the Greek 'privative alpha' (ἀ- as a prefix) which makes a negative by 'depriving' the word of its usual sense.[2] This is particularly common in medical terms, e.g. 'anaemia', 'anhedonia' (see 'ἡδύς') and 'anaesthesia' (see 'αἰσθάνομαι').

Breathings

When looking for derivatives from Greek words beginning with a vowel, it is important to remember the importance of the breathing, which counts as part of the spelling. A 'rough' breathing (ʽ) indicates an 'h' sound before the vowel and a 'smooth' breathing (ʼ) indicates the absence of an 'h' sound. Therefore, 'Ἕλλην' gives us 'Hellenic' and 'ἕξ' gives us the prefix 'hex-', but 'ἀκούω' gives us 'acoustic'. It is worth noting that all words beginning with 'υ' (upsilon) have a rough breathing.

Accents

Accents are included on the GCSE DVL and, for consistency, are therefore also included in this lexicon. However, knowledge

[2] Taylor, *Greek Beyond GCSE* p87.

of accents is not required for the ICCG or the GCSE (or indeed for A Level). For a more detailed explanation of accents and their use, see Taylor, *Greek to GCSE 1* p89. Attention has been drawn to two examples in this lexicon where accents (together with breathings) differentiate otherwise identical words, as some students may find this helpful. See 'εἷς, μία, ἕν' ('one') and the accompanying footnote. See also Taylor, *Greek to GCSE 1* pp98–9 on the uses of τίς/τις and the notes there on accents.

Transliteration of Greek letters

The Greek alphabet is set out in full at the end of this Introduction; the word 'alphabet' itself derives from the names of the first two letters in the Greek alphabet, 'alpha' and 'beta'. It is worth noting the alternative letters in English for some of the Greek symbols. This can be very helpful when considering derivatives. For example, 'κ' (kappa) can be transliterated as 'c' or 'k' in English, hence 'κριτής' ('judge') gives us 'critic'. Likewise, 'υ' (upsilon) can be transliterated as 'u' or 'y' hence 'ὕπνος' ('sleep') gives us 'hypno-' as a prefix (see also the note on breathings above).

Mnemonics and choice of derivatives

Not every Greek word has a derivative in English and these words can be harder for students to learn. Therefore some of the words in this list are accompanied by a suggested mnemonic.

Such mnemonics are simply starting points and students may wish to devise their own.

The lists of derivatives in this lexicon are by no means exhaustive and students may wish to add further words. Students may also be able to find derivatives for some of the Greek words listed without derivatives.

A verb such as 'ἔρχομαι, εἶμι, ἦλθον' does not have very obvious derivatives: 'proselyte' is unlikely to be known by many GCSE students but has been included with an explanatory footnote for interest. However, like many irregular verbs, because 'ἔρχομαι, εἶμι, ἦλθον' is likely to be encountered relatively often in Greek texts, it should soon become familiar.

Derivatives in Greek grammar and literary terms

Many grammatical terms derive from Greek and these have been referred to in the footnotes where possible, e.g. see 'apodosis' in the footnote to 'ἀπό'.

Names of literary devices which students may encounter in commentaries on set texts also often originate from Greek, e.g. 'onomatopoeia', 'polysyndeton', etc. Some of these have been explained in the footnotes together with examples from Greek literature (the translations for which are the author's own). Students may enjoy finding other examples in the texts they are studying. Terms which are likely to be well-known by students, such as 'metaphor' have not been defined or accompanied by examples so students may wish to add their own.

Pronunciation

There is an excellent summary of pronunciation of Greek in Taylor, *Greek to GCSE 1* pp1–2.

Fear of 'cacoepy' ('bad or wrong pronunciation') – see 'κακός' – should, if at all possible, not prevent students from having a go at saying Greek words out loud. Such an exercise can help with memorising vocabulary, as well as being great fun. The sounds of Greek words also give clues as to possible derivatives.

Any opportunity to see a Greek play performed in the original is a wonderful way to enjoy the euphony of the spoken language. Many student productions are now performed around the country, usually with English surtitles. To hear an audience laugh out loud when an actor delivers, in Greek, a line from Aristophanes is not only one of the best forms of catharsis, but also proof that ancient Greek still has a voice in the modern world.

Further Reading / References

The Cambridge Greek Lexicon (Cambridge, 2021).
The Chambers Dictionary (Revised 13th Edition, Chambers Harrap Publishers Ltd., 2016).

Greek to GCSE Parts 1 and 2, John Taylor (Bloomsbury, revised edition 2016).
Greek Beyond GCSE, John Taylor (Bloomsbury, second edition 2017).
Homer's Odyssey I–XII and XIII–XXIV, W. B. Stanford (ed.) (Bristol, 1996).
Homer's Iliad I–XII and XIII–XXIV, M. M. Willcock (ed.) (Bristol, 1996 and 1999).
Oxford Grammar of Classical Greek, James Morwood (Oxford, 2001).

Details of the OCR (Oxford Cambridge and RSA) GCSE specification (including accidence and syntax) for Classical Greek: https://www.ocr.org.uk/Images/220700-specification-accredited-gcse-classical-greek-j292.pdf.
Details of the ICCG specification (including accidence and syntax): https://intermediategreekcert.com/specification/.

Abbreviations

acc	accusative
cf	compare
dat	dative
gen	genitive

The Greek Alphabet

The Greek alphabet has twenty-four letters:

symbol	*name*	*English equivalent*	*pronunciation*
α	alpha	a	short as in *bat* / long as in *father*
β	beta	b	b
γ	gamma	g	as in *get* **
δ	delta	d	d
ε	epsilon	e (short)	as in *get*
ζ	zeta	z, sd	as in *wisdom*
η	eta	e (long)	as in *hair*
θ	theta	th	as in *ant-hill*, or as in *third* †
ι	iota	i	short as in *bit* / long as in *police*
κ	kappa	c, k	k
λ	lambda	l	l
μ	mu	m	m

symbol	*name*	*English equivalent*	*pronunciation*
ν	nu	n	n
ξ	xi	x	x, ks
ο	omicron	o (short)	as in *got*
π	pi	p	p
ρ	rho	r	r
σ/ς*	sigma	s	s
τ	tau	t	t
υ	upsilon	u, y	short as in French *tu* / long as in *sur*
φ	phi	ph	as in *uphold*, or as in *phrase* †
χ	chi	ch	as in *packhorse*, or as in *loch* †
ψ	psi	ps	as in *lapse*
ω	omega	o (long)	between the sounds in *oar* and in *raw*

* σ normally, ς at the end of a word, e.g. 'γλώσσης' (genitive of 'γλῶσσα', meaning 'tongue' or 'language')
** gamma is pronounced as *n* rather than *g* when it comes before another gamma or before a *k* sound (kappa, xi or chi)
† with the aspirated ('breathed-on') consonants theta, phi and chi, the first pronunciation given (like *t*, *p* and *k* with emphatic breathing) represents more accurately the sound in classical times; but the second (with stronger *h* element), standard in later Greek, may be found more convenient in practice (to avoid confusion with the unaspirated tau, pi and kappa).

Greek Lexicon α – ω

GCSE students need to know all the entries in this lexicon other than the 16 entries with a double asterisk **; ICCG students need to know all the entries which are asterisked (whether with one or two asterisks).

Verbs are usually given with present, future, aorist, and aorist passive. Where a particular form (usually the aorist passive) is not shown, it either does not exist or is uncommon and not needed for GCSE. Knowledge of the aorist passive form of verbs is not required for the ICCG.

Nouns are given with nominative, genitive, and article to show gender.[1]

Adjectives are given with masculine, feminine, and neuter.

---

[1] The name of a city or a country is usually feminine.
The proper noun for the people of a city or a country is usually masculine, even when describing a group of people that includes both men and women, regardless of the numbers of each, e.g. a group of twelve women and one man would still be masculine.

α

ἀγαθός, ἀγαθή, ἀγαθόν[2] *

adjective

good

Agatha, agathodaimon

....

ἀγγέλλω, ἀγγελῶ, ἤγγειλα, ἠγγέλθην*

verb

I announce

angel, angel-cake, angelology (cf. λόγος), angelophany (cf. φαίνομαι), angelshark

....

[2] The superlative of 'ἀγαθός' is 'ἄριστος' ('best', 'very good') which gives us words such as 'aristocracy'.

ἄγγελος, ἀγγέλου, ὁ *

noun

messenger

***see* ἀγγέλλω**

ἀγορά, ἀγορᾶς, ἡ *

noun

market-place

agoraphobe (cf.* φόβος*), agoraphobia, category (cf.* κατά*), panegyric

ἀγρός, ἀγροῦ, ὁ *

noun

field, countryside

agrarian, agrichemical, agriculture, agriscience,*[3] *agrobiology (cf. βίος, λόγος), agroecosystem, agroforestry, agroindustry, agronomy (cf. νόμος)

……………………………………………………………

ἄγω, ἄξω, ἤγαγον, ἤχθην *

verb

I lead, bring

agoge,*[4] *apagoge (cf. ἀπό), pedagogue (cf. παῖς), strategy (cf. στρατηγός)

……………………………………………………………

ἀγών, ἀγῶνος, ὁ *

noun

contest, trial

agon,*[5] *agonist,*[6] *agony, antagonist, protagonist

……………………………………………………………

ἀδικέω, ἠδίκησα

verb

I do wrong, injure

……………………………………………………………

---

3 'Science' is a derivative of the Latin verb 'scio' ('I know').

4 In ancient Greek music, 'agoge' is the tempo.

5 In a Greek play (whether tragedy or comedy), the 'agon' is a conflict, or a formal debate, between two characters.

6 In ancient Greece, an 'agonist' was a competitor in public games.

ἄδικος, ἄδικος, ἄδικον

adjective

unjust, wrong

ἀεί *

adverb

always

Ἀθῆναι, Ἀθηνῶν, αἱ *

proper noun

Athens

Ἀθηναῖοι, Ἀθηναίων, οἱ *

proper noun

the Athenians

᾿Αθηναῖος, ᾿Αθηναῖα, ᾿Αθηναῖον *

adjective

Athenian

....

ἆθλον, ἄθλου, τό *

noun

prize, reward

athlete, athletics, heptathlon (cf. ἑπτά), pentathlon (cf. πέντε), triathlon (cf. τρεῖς)

....

αἱρέω, αἱρήσω, εἷλον, ᾑρέθην

verb

I take

....

αἰσθάνομαι, αἰσθήσομαι, ᾐσθόμην

verb

I notice, perceive

aesthesia, aesthesis, aesthetic, anaesthesia,[7] anaesthetic, anaesthesiology (cf. λόγος)

....

αἰσχρός, αἰσχρά, αἰσχρόν

adjective

shameful, ugly, disgraceful

....

αἰτέω, ᾔτησα

verb

I ask, ask for

....

αἴτιος, αἰτία, αἴτιον + gen

adjective

responsible for, guilty of

aetiology[8] (cf. λόγος), aetiological

....

---

[7] See 'Privative alpha' in Introduction.

[8] 'aetiology' is a story or account which explains the origin, or causation, of something, e.g. the story of Persephone and the origin of the seasons.

αἰχμάλωτος, αἰχμαλώτου, ὁ

noun

prisoner (of war)

....

ἀκούω, ἀκούσομαι, ἤκουσα, ἠκούσθην *

verb

I hear, listen (to)

acoustic, acoustics, acousto-electric

....

ἀληθής, ἀληθής, ἀληθές

adjective

true

alethic[9]

....

[9] 'alethic' is a term in philosophy.

ἀλλά *

conjunction
but

……………………………………………………………

ἄλλος, ἄλλη, ἄλλο *

adjective
other, another
allegory, allergy (cf. ἔργον***)***
allo- (combining form signifying 'other') e.g. allograph (cf. γράφω***), allometry, allopathy (cf.*** πάσχω***), allophone (cf.*** φωνή***), allotheism (cf.*** θεός***), allotropy***[10]

……………………………………………………………

ἄν

particle
[in conditional sentence, makes aorist verb mean 'would have …']

……………………………………………………………

[10] 'allotropy' is a term in chemistry.

ἀνά + acc

preposition

up

anabasis[11] ***(cf. βαίνω), anabiosis (cf. βίος), anabolic, anacatharsis, analeptic (cf. λαμβάνω), analysis (cf. λύω), anathema, anatomy, aneurism (cf. εὐρύς)***

....

ἀναγκάζω, ἀναγκάσω, ἠνάγκασα, ἠναγκάσθην

verb

I force, compel

ananke

....

ἀναχωρέω, ἀνεχώρησα

verb

I retreat, withdraw

....

ἀνδρεῖος, ἀνδρεία, ἀνδρεῖον *

adjective

brave, manly

see ἀνήρ

....

---

[11] 'anabasis' literally means a 'going up' or an ascent. Xenophon's *Anabasis* describes the military advance up-country in 401 BC of Cyrus the Younger together with the 'Ten Thousand'. It also describes the army's 'katabasis' meaning a 'going down' or a retreat, following Cyrus' death in battle.

ἄνεμος, ἀνέμου, ὁ *

noun

wind

anemo- (combining form signifying 'wind') e.g. anemogram, anemograph (cf. γράφω), anemology, anemometer, anemone, anemophobia (cf. φόβος)

....

ἄνευ + gen

preposition

without

aneuploid[12]

....

ἀνήρ, ἀνδρός, ὁ

noun

man, husband

andro- or andr- (combining form signifying 'man, male') e.g. androcentric, androcephalous (cf. κεφαλή), androgenous (cf. γίγνομαι), android, andropause (cf. παύω), androphore (cf. φέρω)

....

---

[12] 'aneuploid' is a term in biology.

ἄνθρωπος, ἀνθρώπου, ὁ *

noun

man, person

anthrop- (combining form signifying 'man, human') e.g. anthropobiology (cf. βίος, λόγος), anthropography, anthropology, anthropomorphism, anthroposophist (cf. σοφός)

....

ἄξιος, ἀξία, ἄξιον + gen

adjective

worthy of, deserving

axiology (cf. λόγος), axiologist, axiom, axiomatic

....

ἀπό + gen *

preposition

from, away from

***apagoge (cf. ἄγω), apocalypse, apocope,*[13] *apodosis*[14] *(cf. δίδωμι), apodyterium,*[15] *apology, apophasis (cf. φημί), aposiopesis,*[16] *apostrophe,*[17] *apotheosis (cf. θεός), apotropaic*[18]**

....

ἀποβάλλω, ἀπέβαλον *

verb

I throw away

see βάλλω

....

---

[13] By 'apocope' final vowels are sometimes lost in prepositions, e.g. 'παρά' becomes 'πάρ' (see footnote on 'euphony' under 'φωνή').

[14] The 'apodosis' is the main clause of a conditional sentence, expressing the consequence (i.e. not the 'if' half, which is the 'protasis'). 'Apodosis' literally means 'giving back', i.e. providing an answer. The 'protasis' usually comes before the 'apodosis' but (in both Greek and English) can come after it. (Taylor, *Greek to GCSE 2* p188.)

[15] An 'apodyterium' was an undressing-room at Roman baths.

[16] 'aposiopesis' is a literary device in which the speaker stops before completing the sentence, e.g. 'εἴ περ γάρ κ' ἐθέλῃσιν Ὀλύμπιος ἀστεροπητὴς | ἐξ ἑδέων στυφελίξαι...' (Homer, *Iliad* 1.580-1), ('for if the Olympian lightning-sender wishes to smash us from our seats...'). Here something like 'what can we do about it?' must be understood. (For all of this footnote: Morwood p235.)

[17] 'Apostrophe' is a literary term meaning the author 'turns away' from his story (usually being narrated in the third person) to address a particular character directly. In the *Iliad*, Homer directly addresses Patroclus 8 times and Menelaus 7 times. (Stanford, vol. 2 p218.) Some editors suggest it demonstrates Homer's affection for these characters. An example is: 'ἔνθα κέ τοι, Μενέλαε, φάνη βιότοιο τελευτὴ | Ἕκτορος ἐν παλάμῃσιν, ἐπεὶ πολὺ φέρτερος ἦεν,' ('Then, Menelaus, the end of your life would have materialised, at the hands of Hektor, since he was much mightier,'). (*Iliad* 7.104-5.)

[18] 'apotropaic' literally means 'a turning from' or 'turning aside' and describes symbols (such as an image of Medusa) which were variously used in the ancient world with the purpose of warding off evil.

ἀποθνῄσκω, ἀποθανοῦμαι, ἀπέθανον *

verb

I die, am killed

see **θάνατος**

....

ἀποκρίνομαι, ἀποκρινοῦμαι, ἀπεκρινάμην

verb

I reply, answer

apocrine[19]

....

ἀποκτείνω, ἀποκτενῶ, ἀπέκτεινα *

verb

I kill

....

[19] 'apocrine' is a term in biology.

ἄρα; *

particle

[*introduces a question*]

....

ἀρχή, ἀρχῆς, ἡ

noun

beginning, rule, power, empire

anarchy, arch- (prefix meaning 'first' or 'chief') e.g. archangel (cf. ἀγγέλλω), arch-enemy, archetype, architect, architrave, archive, arch-poet, arch-villain[20]

....

ἄρχω, ἦρξα + gen

verb

I rule

-archy (combining form signifying 'government of a particular type') e.g. matriarchy (cf. μήτηρ), monarchy (cf. μόνος), oligarchy (cf. ὀλίγοι), patriarchy (cf. πατήρ)

....

ἄρχομαι, ἠρξάμην + gen

verb

I begin

see ἀρχή for examples of arch- (prefix meaning 'first' or 'chief')

....

---

[20] The prefix 'arch-' may be used to emphasise an already derogatory epithet.

ἄρχων, ἄρχοντος , ὁ *

noun

ruler, magistrate

-arch (combining form signifying 'chief, ruler') e.g. ecclesiarch (cf. ἐκκλησία), matriarch (cf. μήτηρ), monarch (cf. μόνος), oligarch (cf. ὀλίγοι), patriarch (cf. πατήρ)

……………………………………………………………

ἀσθενής, ἀσθενής, ἀσθενές

adjective

weak

asthenia, asthenic, asthenosphere[21]

……………………………………………………………

ἀσπίς, ἀσπίδος, ἡ

noun

shield

aspidistra,[22] ***aspidium,***[23] ***aspidioid***

……………………………………………………………

ἀσφαλής, ἀσφαλής, ἀσφαλές

adjective

safe

……………………………………………………………

---

[21] 'asthenosphere' is a term in geology.

[22] An 'aspidistra' is an evergreen plant with shield-like long, tough leaves.

[23] 'aspidium' and 'aspidioid' are terms in botany.

αὖθις *

adverb

again, in turn

....

αὐτός, αὐτή, αὐτό *

pronoun

self, himself, herself, itself (*emphatic*)

autism, auto- (combining form signifying 'self') e.g. autobiography (cf. βίος, γράφω), autochthon,[24] autocrat, autodidactic (cf. διδάσκω), autograph, automatic, automobile, autonomy (cf. νόμος), autonym (cf. ὄνομα), autophoby, autopsy, autosave

....

ὁ αὐτός, ἡ αὐτή, τὸ αὐτό *

pronoun

the same

auto- (combining form signifying 'same') e.g. autocorrelation, autograft (cf. γράφω), autologous, autotype, autotypography, tautology[25]

....

[24] An 'autochthon' means a primitive inhabitant of a country. It means 'sprung from the soil' from the Greek words for 'self' and 'soil'. According to mythology, the original Athenians sprang from the soil.

[25] 'tautology' is a literary term describing the use of two words or phrases with almost the same meaning, usually for emphasis, e.g. 'τελευτήσῃς τε καὶ ἔρξῃς', ('completed and done') (Homer, *Odyssey* 1.293.)

αὐτόν, αὐτήν, αὐτό (acc/gen/dat only – also plural) *

pronoun

him, her, it, them

....

ἀφικνέομαι, ἀφίξομαι, ἀφικόμην

verb

I arrive

....

β

βαίνω, βήσομαι, ἔβην *
(Aorist tense not needed for the ICCG)

verb

I go

acrobat, anabasis (cf. ἀνά and corresponding footnote), base, baseball, baseless, baseline, basement, base rate, basis, hyperbaton,[26] katabasis (cf. footnote to ἀνά), metabasis (cf. μετά), parabasis[27]

....

[26] 'hyperbaton' is a figure of speech in which the usual order of words is reversed. Yoda in *Star Wars* is well-known for this form of speech.

[27] In Greek comedy the 'parabasis' is a speech in which the chorus moves forward to address the audience.

βάλλω, βαλῶ, ἔβαλον, ἐβλήθην *

verb

I throw, fire at, hit (with missile)

amphibology, anabolic (cf. ἀνά), ***ballista,***[28] ***ballistic, bolometer, Discobolos,***[29] ***hyperbole,***[30] ***parable, peribolos, pyroballogy (cf.*** πῦρ***)***

....

βάρβαροι, βαρβάρων, οἱ

noun

foreigners, barbarians, non-Greek

Barbara, barbarian, barbaric, barbarous

....

---

[28] A 'ballista' is a Roman military weapon for throwing heavy missiles.

[29] Myron's 'Discobolos' ('discus thrower') is one of the best known sculptures from the ancient world. Myron's original bronze (*c.* 450 BC), does not survive but several marble copies produced in the Roman period still exist. (See further: *The Discobolus*, Ian Jenkins (The British Museum Press, 2012).)

[30] 'hyperbole' means excessive exaggeration.

βασιλεύς, βασιλέως, ὁ

noun

king

basilica, basilican, basilicon, basilisk

βία, βίας, ἡ

noun

force, strength

βίβλος, βίβλου, ἡ *

noun

book

bible, bibliography (cf. γράφω), bibliomania, bibliophile (cf. φιλέω), bibliopegy, bibliophagist (cf. ἐσθίω)

βίος, βίου, ὁ *

noun

life

amphibious, anabiosis (cf. ἀνά), anaerobic, antibiotic bio- (combining form signifying 'life' or 'living organisms') e.g. bioastronautics, biochemistry, biodegradable, biodiversity, bioengineer, biology (cf. λόγος), biography (cf. γράφω), bionic, biopic, biopsy

....

βλάπτω, ἔβλαψα *

verb

I harm, damage

....

βοάω, ἐβόησα[31]

verb

I shout

....

βοή, βοῆς, ἡ *

noun

shout

see βοάω

....

[31] A possible way to remember 'βοάω' is by likening it, in sound and meaning, to the word 'bellow'.

βοηθέω, ἐβοήθησα + dat

verb

I help, come to help

....

βουλή, βουλῆς, ἡ *

noun

plan, a council

boule,*[32] *probouleutic (cf. πρό)

....

βούλομαι, βουλήσομαι, ἐβουλήθην

verb

I wish

....

βραδύς, βραδεῖα, βραδύ

adjective

slow

brady- (combining form signifying 'slow') e.g. bradycardia, bradypeptic, bradyseism

....

[32] The 'boule' is the parliament of modern Greece.

γ

γάρ[33] *
particle
for

....

γε[34]
particle
at any rate, even, at least

....

γελάω, γελάσομαι, ἐγέλασα
verb
I laugh
gelastic

....

[33] Comes second word in sentence, clause or phrase.
[34] Comes second word in sentence, clause or phrase.

γέρων, γέροντος, ὁ *

noun

old man

geriatric, geriatrics, geriatrician (cf.* ἰατρός*)

....

γῆ, γῆς, ἡ *

noun

land, earth

geo- (combining form signifying 'earth') e.g. geocentric, geology, geography, geometry, geophysics, geopolitics (cf.* πόλις*)

....

γίγας, γίγαντος, ὁ **

noun

giant

gigantic, giganticide, gigantology, gigantomachy (cf.* μάχη*; cf.* θεός *and corresponding footnote)

....

γίγνομαι, γενήσομαι, ἐγενόμην

verb

I become, happen, occur
androgenous (cf. ἀνήρ), eugenic (cf. εὖ), genesis
-gen (combining form signifying 'producing' or 'produced') e.g. oxygen, (or 'growth') e.g. endogen

……………………………………………………………………

γιγνώσκω, γνώσομαι, ἔγνων, ἐγνώσθην *

(Aorist tense not needed for the ICCG)

verb

I know, realise, understand
agnostic, gnomon,[35] gnosis
-gnosis (combining form signifying 'knowledge' or 'recognition') e.g. diagnosis, prognosis (cf. πρό)

……………………………………………………………………

γλῶσσα, γλώσσης, ἡ

noun

tongue, language
gloss- or glosso-, sometimes glotto- (combining form signifying 'tongue' or 'language') e.g. glossitis, glossology, glottochronology (cf. χρόνος)
gloss, glossary, monoglot, polyglot

……………………………………………………………………

---

[35] 'gnomon' is a term in geometry. A gnomon is also the part of a sundial that casts a shadow enabling us to 'know' the time.

γράφω, ἔγραψα *

verb

I write, draw

geography (cf.* γῆ*), graffiti, graph, graphic, graphite

-graph (combining form signifying a device that writes or records) e.g. photograph, seismograph, telegraph, (or signifying the thing written) e.g. autograph (cf.* αὐτος*), monograph (cf.* μόνος*)

....

γυνή, γυναικός, ἡ

noun

woman, wife

gyn-, gynaeco-, gyno- or -gyny (combining form signifying 'female' or 'woman') e.g. gynaecoid, gynaecology, gynaecocracy, gynophobia, misogyny

....

δ

δακρύω, ἐδάκρυσα

verb

I cry, weep

lachrymal (also lacrymal),*[36] *lachrymal duct, lachrymose

....

δέ[37] *

particle

but, and

....

δεῖ, δεήσει, ἐδέησε with acc + infinitive

impersonal verb

it is necessary

....

---

36 'lachrymal' derives from 'lachryma', a medieval spelling of the Latin 'lacrima' meaning 'tear' (as in 'cry'). The Greek word for 'tear', 'δάκρυμα', may have influenced the spelling because of the 'υ' (upsilon) which can be transliterated as 'y'. (Chambers p854.) 'Lacryma Christi' (literally, 'Christ's tear') is a wine made from grapes on Mount Vesuvius.

37 Comes second word in sentence, clause or phrase.

δεινός, δεινή, δεινόν *

adjective

terrible, strange, clever

dino- or deino- (combining form signifying 'huge' or 'terrible') e.g. dinosaur, dinomania, dinoturbation

....

δεῖπνον, δείπνου, τό *

noun

dinner, meal

deipnosophist[38]

....

[38] A 'deipnosophist' is someone whose dinner-table conversation is erudite. The term derives from *Deipnosophistai*, the title of a work by Athenaeus (*c.* AD 200).

δέκα *

cardinal number

ten

deca- (combining form signifying 'ten') e.g. decade, decagon, decagram, decahedron, decalitre, decamerous, decane,[39] decapod (cf. πούς), decastyle,[40] decasyllable, decathlon (cf. ἆθλον)

....

δένδρον, δένδρου, τό *

noun

tree

dendr- or dendro- (combining form signifying 'tree') e.g. dendriform, dendrite, dendritic,[41] dendrochronology (cf. χρόνος), dendroclimatology, dendrogram, rhododendron

....

δεσμωτήριον, δεσμωτηρίου, το **

noun

prison

....

---

[39] 'decane' is a term in chemistry.

[40] 'decastyle' means a building or portico with ten columns in front, or a group of ten pillars.

[41] A 'dendritic drainage pattern' is a term in geology.

δεσπότης, δεσπότου, ὁ

noun

master

despot, despotic, despotocracy

……………………………………………………………

δεύτερος, δευτέρα, δεύτερον *

ordinal number

second

deuter- (combining form signifying 'second') e.g. deuteragonist,[42] deuteranopia,[43] deuterium, deuterogamy, deuteroplasm, deuteroscopy

……………………………………………………………

δέχομαι, δέξομαι, ἐδεξάμην

verb

I receive, welcome

pandect, pandectist, synecdoche[44]

……………………………………………………………

δή

particle

indeed

……………………………………………………………

---

[42] A 'deuteragonist' is an actor who plays a secondary character in a Greek play.

[43] 'deuteranopia' is a form of colour blindness in which green and red are confused.

[44] 'synecdoche' is a literary expression in which the part is used to describe the whole, e.g. Homer uses 'δόρυ' ('shaft of a spear') also to mean 'spear'.

δῆμος, δήμου, ὁ *

noun

people, community

deme,*[45] *democracy, demography, demology, demotic, epidemic, pandemic

....

διά + acc *

preposition

because of, on account of

diagnosis (cf. γιγνώσκω)

....

διὰ τί; *

prepositional phrase

why?

....

διά + gen *

preposition

through

dialect (cf. λέγω), dialogue (cf. λόγος)

....

---

[45] 'deme' is a term in biology. A 'deme' was a village or district representing the smallest political constituency in the Athenian democratic system.

δι᾽ ὀλίγου

prepositional phrase
soon

....

διαφθείρω, διαφθερῶ, διέφθειρα, διεφθάρην

verb
I destroy, corrupt

....

διδάσκαλος, διδασκάλου, ὁ **

noun
teacher
***see* διδάσκω**

....

διδάσκω, διδάξω, ἐδίδαξα, ἐδιδάχθην *

verb
I teach, tell
autodidactic (cf.* αὐτος*), didactic, didactics

....

(δίδωμι), δώσω, ἔδωκα

verb
I give (*future and aorist indicative active and infinitives only*)
anecdote, antidote, apodosis (cf.* ἀπό *and corresponding footnote), dosage, dose, dosemeter, dosology

....

δίκαιος, δικαία, δίκαιον

adjective

just, fair, upright

dikast[46]

....

διότι *

conjunction

because

....

διώκω, ἐδίωξα *

verb

I chase, pursue, prosecute

....

δοκεῖ (μοι), δόξει, ἔδοξε

impersonal verb

(I) decide (= it seems good (to me))

doxographer, doxy, heterodox, orthodoxy, paradox (cf. παρά)

....

[46] A 'dikast' is the word taken directly from the Greek word with the same root as 'δίκαιος', referring to a citizen who was both judge and juror in the Athenian court system.

δοῦλος, δούλου, ὁ *

noun

slave

doula, douleia, doulocracy, dulia, dulosis, dulotic, hierodule (cf. ἱερός and corresponding footnote)

....

δοῦναι (cf. δίδωμι)

verb

to give, to have given (*aorist infinitive*)

***see* δίδωμι**

....

δύο, δύο, δύο *

cardinal number

two

duet, duo (cf. 'duo' in Latin), duodecimal, duopoly

....

δυστυχής, δυστυχής, δυστυχές

adjective

unlucky

***see* τύχη**

....

δῶρον, δώρου, τό *

noun

present, gift

Dorothy, Pandora, Theodore

....

ε

ἐάν

conjunction and particle

if

....

ἑαυτόν, ἑαυτήν, ἑαυτό

reflexive pronoun

himself, herself, itself, (plural) themselves (reflexive)

....

ἐγώ, ἐμοῦ/μου *

pronoun

I, (*acc, etc.*) me

ego (cf. 'ego' in Latin), egocentric, egoism, egomaniac, egotism, ego-surfing[47]

....

[47] 'ego-surfing' means searching for one's own name on the Internet.

ἐμός, ἐμή, ἐμόν *

possessive adjective

my

....

ἐθέλω, ἐθελήσω, ἠθέλησα *

verb

I wish, am willing

....

εἰ

conjunction

if

....

εἰδέναι (cf. οἶδα)

verb

to know

....

εἰδώς, εἰδυῖα, εἰδός, (cf. οἶδα)

participle

knowing

....

εἶδον[48] *

verb (irregular aorist)

I saw

....

εἰμί, ἔσομαι, ἦν (imperfect) * (Present and imperfect tenses only for the ICCG)

verb (irregular)

I am

....

εἶμι (cf. ἔρχομαι)

verb

I shall go

....

---

[48] GCSE candidates: see also ὁράω.

εἰρήνη, εἰρήνης, ἡ *

noun

peace

eirenic, eirenicon, Irene

εἰς + acc *

preposition

to, into

***see footnote to* εἷς, μία, ἕν**

εἰς τοσοῦτον

prepositional phrase

to such an extent

εἷς, μία, ἕν[49] *

cardinal number

one

hendiadys[50]

....

εἰσβάλλω, εἰσέβαλον

verb

I throw into, invade

....

εἰσπίπτω, εἰσέπεσον *

verb

I fall into

***see* πίπτω**

....

---

[49] The breathing (and accent, or absence of it) distinguish between 'εἷς' meaning 'one' (masculine nominative) and 'εἰς' meaning 'into' (preposition + accusative). The breathing (and accent, or absence of it) also distinguish between 'ἕν' meaning 'one' (neuter nominative/accusative) and 'ἐν' meaning 'in' (preposition + dative). The context of a sentence will usually avoid any ambiguity in any event. (Taylor, *Greek to GCSE 1* p145.)

[50] 'hendiadys' is a rhetorical device in which a single idea is expressed through two nouns or verbs, or in which a notion, normally expressible by an adjective and a noun, is expressed by two nouns joined by 'and' or another conjunction, e.g. 'ἐν ἁλὶ κύμασί τε' 'in the sea and the waves' (for 'in the waves of the sea'). (Euripides, *Helen* 226.) 'Hendiadys' literally means 'one by means of two'. (Morwood p237.)

ἐκ (ἐξ before vowel) + gen *

preposition

out of, from

ekphrasis,*[51] *ex (cf. 'ex' in Latin) e.g. ex warehouse, exhale, exit, exude

....

ἕκαστος, ἑκάστη, ἕκαστον *

adjective

each

....

ἐκβαίνω, ἐξέβην * (Aorist tense not needed for the ICCG)

verb

I go out

***see* βαίνω**

....

ἐκεῖ *

adverb

there

....

---

51 'ekphrasis' is a literary or rhetorical description of a work of art. A good example is the description of Achilles' shield in Homer's *Iliad* 18.

ἐκεῖνος, ἐκείνη, ἐκεῖνο

demonstrative pronoun

that, *plural* those

ἐκκλησία, ἐκκλησίας, ἡ[52] *

noun

assembly, meeting

ecclesiarch (cf. ἄρχων), ecclesiastical, ecclesiology

[52] A possible way to remember 'ἐκκλησία' is by likening it, in sound and meaning, to the word 'class'.

ἐκτρέχω, ἐξέδραμον *

verb

I run out

see **τρέχω**

....

ἐκφεύγω, ἐξέφυγον

verb

I escape

see **φεύγω**

....

ἐλεύθερος, ἐλευθέρα, ἐλεύθερον *

adjective

free

eleutherarch (cf. **ἄρχων*****), eleutherian, eleutherodactyl, eleutheromania, eleutherophobia (cf.*** **φόβος*****)***

....

Ἑλλάς, Ἑλλάδος, ἡ *

proper noun

Greece

Helladic

....

῞Ελλην, ῞Ελληνος, ὁ *

proper noun

a Greek, Greek man

Hellene, Hellenic, Hellenise, Hellenist, Hellenophile (cf. φιλέω), philhellenic

....

ἐλπίζω, ἐλπιῶ, ἤλπισα

verb

I hope, expect

....

ἐμβάλλω, ἐνέβαλον *

verb

I throw in, thrust in

see βάλλω

....

ἐν + dat *

preposition

in, among

see footnote to εἷς, μία, ἕν

en- (in words derived from Greek, used to form words with sense of 'in') e.g. enarthrosis, encaustic (cf. καίω and corresponding footnote), encephalon (cf. κεφαλή), enclitic,[53] encyclopaedia (cf. παῖς)

....

[53] 'enclitic' means a word that cannot stand alone but closely follows another word (e.g. the indefinite adjective/pronoun 'τις'). (Taylor, *Greek to GCSE 2* p324.)

ἐνθάδε *

adverb

here, there

....

ἐννέα *

cardinal number

nine

ennea- (combining form signifying 'nine') e.g. ennead, enneagon, enneagram, enneahedron, enneastyle (cf. δέκα and corresponding footnote)

....

ἔνοικος, ἐνοίκου, ὁ

noun

inhabitant

....

ἕξ *

cardinal number

six

hex- (combining form signifying 'six') e.g. hexad, hexadactylic, hexadecimal, hexaëmeron (cf. ἡμέρα), hexafoil, hexagon, hexagram, hexahedron, hexameter,[54] ***hexastyle (cf. δέκα and corresponding footnote)***

....

ἐξάγω, ἐξήγαγον *

verb

I lead out

see ἄγω

....

ἔξεστι(ν) (μοι)

impersonal verb

I am allowed, I can (= it is permitted to me/possible for me)

....

ἐπεί *

conjunction

when, since

....

---

[54] A 'hexameter' is a line of verse having six measures or 'feet'. Homer's epic poems, the *Iliad* and the *Odyssey* are composed in 'dactylic hexameters'. (See further: Taylor, *Greek Beyond GCSE* p208.)

ἔπειτα *

adverb

then, afterwards

....

ἐπί + acc

preposition

against, onto, on, at

epi- or ep- (prefix meaning 'on') e.g. epibenthos, epicentre, epidemic, epidermis, epigram, epigraph, epilepsy (cf. λαμβάνω), epilithic (cf. λίθος), epilogue, episode, epitaph, epitasis,[55] epithet,[56] epitome

....

ἐπιστολή, ἐπιστολῆς, ἡ *

noun

letter

epistle, epistolarian, epistolet, epistolise

....

ἕπομαι, ἕψομαι, ἑσπόμην + dat

verb

I follow

....

[55] The 'epitasis' is the main action of a Greek drama building up to the catastrophe, as opposed to the 'protasis' which is the initial part of a drama.

[56] Cf. the entries under καλός, νίκη and οὐρανός for some examples of epithets given to Greek goddesses.

ἑπτά *

cardinal number

seven

hepta- (combining form signifying 'seven') e.g. heptachord,*[57] *heptad, heptagon, heptahedron, heptamerous, heptameter, heptapodic (cf.* πούς*), heptarchy (cf.* ἄρχω*), heptasyllabic, heptathlon (cf.* ἆθλον*), heptatonic

....

ἔργον, ἔργου, τό *

noun

work, task, deed, action

allergy (cf.* ἄλλος*), argon,*[58] *dramaturgy, energy (cf.* ἐν*), ergogram, ergomania, ergonomics, ergophobia, ergate,*[59] *hierurgy (cf.* ἱερός*), metallurgy, synergy

....

ἔρχομαι, εἶμι, ἦλθον * (Aorist tense only for the ICCG)

verb

I go, come

proselyte,*[60] *proselytise

....

---

[57] In Greek music, a 'heptachord' is a series of tones and semitones spanning the interval of a seventh.

[58] 'argon' is formed from privative alpha (see Introduction) and ἔργον indicating its inactive, or inert nature. It is a colourless, odourless, inert gaseous element (symbol Ar on the periodic table).

[59] An 'ergate' is a worker ant.

[60] A 'proselyte' is someone who has converted from one religion or doctrine to another.

ἐρωτάω, ἐρωτήσω, ἠρόμην (*or* ἠρώτησα)

verb

I ask (a question)

erotema, eroteme, erotesis, erotetic

....

ἐσθίω, (ἔδομαι), ἔφαγον * (Present and aorist tenses only for the ICCG)

verb

I eat

aphagia, edible (cf. 'edo' meaning 'I eat' in Latin), oesophagus, -phaga, -phage or -phagous (combining form signifying 'eaters' or 'eating') e.g. hippophagous (cf. ἵππος), phagocyte, phagophobia

....

ἑσπέρα, ἑσπέρας, ἡ[61] *

noun

evening

Hesper,[62] ***Hesperian, hesperid, Hesperides,***[63] ***Hesperis***[64]

....

---

61 In modern Greek 'καλησπέρα' means 'good evening'.

62 'Hesper' is Venus as the evening star.

63 The 'Hesperides' were the 'daughters of the evening' who guarded a tree of golden apples in a garden in the far west, helped by a dragon. Heracles gathered these for his twelfth labour, with the help of Atlas.

64 'Hesperis' is the name of a genus (group) of flowering plants which are fragrant in the evening.

ἔτι *

adverb

still, yet

....

ἑτοῖμος, ἑτοίμη, ἑτοῖμον *

adjective

ready

....

ἔτος, ἔτους, τό

noun

year

trieteric (cf.* τρεῖς*)

....

εὖ

adverb

well

eucalyptus, eucrite, eucryphia, eudaemonism, eugenic (cf.* γίγνομαι*), euharmonic, eulogy, euphemism*[65] *(cf.* φημί*), euphony (cf.* φωνή*), euphorbia, euphoria, eutrophy

....

---

65 'euphemism' is a mild or kindly-cloaked way of saying something which may be thought to be too harsh or blunt, e.g.: 'Εὐμενίδες' ('the kindly ones') for the Furies.

εὐθύς *

adverb

immediately, at once

....

εὑρίσκω, εὑρήσω, ηὗρον, ηὑρέθην *

verb

I find

eureka[66]

....

εὐρύς, εὐρεῖα, εὐρύ

adjective

wide, broad

aneurism (cf. ἀνά), euryhaline, Eurypterus, eurytherm, eurytopic

....

εὐτυχής, εὐτυχής, εὐτυχές

adjective

lucky, fortunate

***see* τύχη**

....

---

66 Archimedes, a Greek scientist and mathematician, is reported to have run into the street crying 'Heureka!' ('I have found it!') after making an important discovery in his bath.

ἔφη (cf. φήμι)

verb

he/she said (*with direct speech*)

....

ἐχθρός, ἐχθρά, ἐχθρόν *

adjective

hostile

....

ἐχθρός, ἐχθροῦ, ὁ *

noun

(personal) enemy (cf. **πολέμιοι**)

....

ἔχω (***imperfect*** **εἶχον), ἕξω, ἔσχον** *

verb

I have

cachexia (cf. **κακός*)***

....

ἕως

conjunction and adverb

while, until

....

ζ

Ζεύς, Διός, ὁ *

proper noun

Zeus

deification, deify, deity (cf. 'deus' meaning 'god' in Latin)

....

ζητέω

verb

I seek

zetetic

....

η

ἤ

conjunction

or, than

....

ἤ … ἤ

conjunction

either … or

....

ἡγεμών, ἡγεμόνος, ὁ

noun

guide, leader

hegemonic, hegemonist, hegemony

....

ἤδη

adverb

already, by now

....

ἡδύς, ἡδεῖα, ἡδύ

adjective

pleasant, sweet

anhedonia, hedonic, hedonism, hedonistic, hedyphane

....

ἡμεῖς, ἡμῶν *

pronoun

we, (*acc, etc.*) us

....

ἡμέτερος, ἡμετέρα, ἡμέτερον *

possessive adjective

our

....

ἡμέρα, ἡμέρας, ἡ[67] *

noun

day

hemeralopia, Hemerobaptist, Hemerocallis, hexaëmeron (cf. ἕξ)

....

[67] In modern Greek 'καλημέρα' means 'good day' or 'good morning'.

θ

θάλασσα, θαλάσσης, ἡ *

noun

sea

thalassaemia, thalassian, thalassic, thalassocracy, thalassographic, thalassotherapy

....

θάνατος, θανάτου, ὁ *

noun

death

thanatism, thanato- (combining form signifying 'death') e.g. thanatognomic (cf. γιγνώσκω), thanatography, thanatoid, thanatology, thanatophobia

....

θάπτω, θάψω, ἔθαψα *

verb

I bury

taphonomy, taphophobia

....

θαυμάζω, ἐθαύμασα *

verb

I am amazed at, admire

thaumato- or thaumat- (combining form signifying 'wonder' or 'miracle') e.g. thaumatogeny, thaumatography, thaumatolatry, thaumatology, thaumatrope, thaumaturge (cf.* ἔργον*)

θεά, θεᾶς, ἡ *

noun

goddess

***see* θεός**

θεός, θεοῦ, ὁ *

noun

god

apotheosis, atheist, theo- (combining form signifying 'god') e.g. Theobroma,[68] theocentric, theocracy, theolinguistics, theology, theomachy[69] (cf. μάχη), theomancy, theopathy (cf. πάσχω), theophany (cf. φαίνομαι), theopneusty

....

Θῆβαι, Θηβῶν, αἱ **

noun

Thebes

....

θυγάτηρ, θυγατρός, ἡ

noun

daughter

....

---

[68] 'Theobroma' is a genus (group) of flowering plants including the cocoa tree, 'Theobroma cacao', the beans of which are used to make chocolate. Theobroma means 'food of the gods'.

[69] A 'theomachy' is a war among or against the gods in Greek mythology, such as the gigantomachy. Book 20 of Homer's *Iliad* is traditionally known under the title *Theomachia;* it opens with a scene on Olympos in which Zeus permits the gods to take part in the battle.

θύρα, θύρας, ἡ[70] *

noun

door

thyratron, thyristor, Thyrostraca

....

θύω, ἔθυσα

verb

I sacrifice

thurible, thurifer, thurify, thyme, thymol (cf. 'thus' meaning 'frankincense' in Latin)

....

[70] A possible way to remember 'θύρα' is by the phrase 'through a door' and the rhyming of 'through' and 'θύρα'.

ι

ἰατρός, ἰατροῦ, ὁ

noun

doctor

-iatric (combining form signifying 'medical care or treatment') e.g. geriatric (cf. γέρων), paediatric (cf. παῖς), psychiatric, iatrochemistry, iatrogenic (cf. γίγνομαι)

....

ἰέναι (cf. εἶμι)

verb

to go

....

ἱερόν, ἱεροῦ, τό *

noun

temple

***see* ἱερός**

....

ἱερός, ἱερά, ἱερόν

adjective

sacred, holy

hierocracy, hierodule*[71] *(cf.* δοῦλος*), hieroglyph, hierogram, hierolatry, hieromancy, hierophant, hierophobia, hierurgy (cf.* ἔργον*)

....

ἵνα + subjunctive or optative

conjunction

in order that, in order to

....

ἱππεύς, ἱππέως, ὁ

noun

cavalryman, *in plural* (the) cavalry

***hippeastrum,*[72] *see* ἵππος**

....

---

71 In ancient Greece and Rome, a 'hierodule' was a group of slaves working in a temple.

72 'hippeastrum' is the name of a genus (group) of plants, including the Amaryllis. It is possible that the name was given due to the flowers resembling a horse's head.

ἵππος, ἵππου, ὁ *

noun

horse

hipp- or hippo- (combining form meaning 'horse') e.g. hippiatric (cf. ἰατρός), hippic, hippocampus, hippodrome, hippophagy (cf. ἐσθίω), hippophile, hippophobe, hippopotamus (cf. ποταμός)

....

ἰσχυρός, ἰσχυρά, ἰσχυρόν

adjective

strong

....

ἰών, ἰοῦσα, ἰόν (ἰοντ-) (cf. εἶμι)

participle

going

....

κ

καθεύδω, *imperfect* ἐκάθευδον *or* καθηῦδον

verb

I sleep

....

καθίζω, καθιῶ, ἐκάθισα

verb

I (make to) sit down

akathisia, cathisma

....

καί *

conjunction

and, also, even, too

....

καίπερ *

conjunction

although, despite (+ *participle*)

....

καίω, καύσω, ἔκαυσα, ἐκαύθην

verb

I burn, set on fire

caustic, caustic soda, cauterise, encaustic[73]

....

κακός, κακή, κακόν[74] *

adjective

bad, wicked, cowardly

cachaemia, cachexia (cf. ἔχω), cacodemon, cacodoxy, cacoepy,[75] ***'cacoethes loquendi',***[76] ***'cacoethes scribendi',***[77] ***cacology, cacophony, cacotrophy***

....

[73] 'encaustic' is a method of decorating e.g. pottery and statues by burning the colours in. An example of an Etruscan statue that was decorated using the encaustic technique is at the British Museum. It dates to 570 BC–560 BC and depicts a woman wearing a long tunic with traces of painted border at the hem, and sandals which were originally painted red. There are traces of blue and yellow on the lotus pattern border of her cloak. The statue was probably influenced by Greek prototypes (cf. πρῶτος), particularly from Crete and the Peloponnese. (https://www.britishmuseum.org/collection/object/G_1850-0227-1.)

[74] The superlative of 'κακός' is 'κάκιστος' ('worst', 'very bad') which gives us words such as 'kakistocracy'.

[75] 'cacoepy' means bad or wrong pronunciation.

[76] 'cacoethes loquendi' means an uncontrollable desire for talking, especially for giving speeches, literally 'a bad habit for speaking'. The 'loquendi' derives from the Latin verb 'loquor' ('I speak').

[77] 'cacoethes scribendi' means an uncontrollable desire for writing or getting one's work into print, literally 'a bad habit for writing'. The 'scribendi' derives from the Latin verb 'scribo' ('I write').

καλέω, καλῶ, ἐκάλεσα, ἐκλήθην

verb

I call, summon

....

κάλλιστος, καλλίστη, κάλλιστον *

adjective

very fine, very beautiful

***see* καλός**

....

καλός, καλή, καλόν *

adjective

beautiful, handsome, fine

Callicarpa,*[78] *calligraphy, callipygian,*[79] *kaleidophone, kaleidoscope, kallitype

....

[78] 'Callicarpa' is a genus (form) of Japanese and Chinese shrubs and small trees, known for beautiful berries and autumn foliage.

[79] 'callipygian' is an epithet of Aphrodite (or Venus) meaning 'with beautiful buttocks'. A marble statue of 'Venus Callipyge' believed to be a Roman copy of a Greek original, is on display in the National Archaeological Museum of Naples. (https://www.museoarcheologiconapoli.it/en/portfolio-item/farnese-collection/.)

κατά + acc

preposition

according to, by, down, along

catheter, cathode, catalogue, category (cf. ἀγορά), katabasis (cf. βαίνω and cf. footnote to ἀνά)

....

κατὰ γῆν

prepositional phrase

by land

....

κατὰ θάλασσαν

prepositional phrase

by sea

....

κατά + gen

preposition

down, down from

***see* κατά + acc**

....

κελεύω, ἐκέλευσα *

verb

I order

proceleusmatic (cf. πρό)

....

κεφαλή, κεφαλῆς, ἡ

noun

head

cephal- or cephalo- (combining form signifying 'head')
e.g. cephalalgia, cephalate, cephalitis, cephalopod[80]
(cf. πούς), hydrocephalus (cf. ὕδωρ)

....

κίνδυνος, κινδύνου, ὁ[81] *

noun

danger

....

---

[80] A cephalopod is a member of the Cephalopoda, or molluscs. They are exclusively marine animals (including cuttlefish, squid, octopus, etc.) with a prominent head and their 'feet' have become modified into arms or tentacles.

[81] A suggestion for remembering 'κίνδυνος' is that it sounds like 'kindle' meaning 'set fire to', which has an element of danger.

κλέπτω, κλέψω, ἔκλεψα, ἐκλάπην *

verb

I steal

kleptocracy, kleptomania

....

κολάζω, ἐκόλασα

verb

I punish

....

κόπτω, κόψω, ἔκοψα

verb

I cut (down)

coppice, copse

....

κόρη, κόρης, ἡ[82] **

noun

girl

....

---

[82] Classical archaeologists use the word 'kore' (plural: 'korai') to describe a statue of a young woman used to mark graves or, more often, as a votive offering to the gods in the sixth and fifth centuries BC. One of the most famous examples of this type of sculpture is the 'Peplos Kore', dating to around 530 BC, excavated on the Acropolis in Athens in 1886. She is on display in the Acropolis Museum in Athens. (https://www.theacropolismuseum.gr/en/statue-kore-peplos-kore.) A 'peplos' is a type of dress worn by women in Greece *c.* 500 BC. There are also two plaster casts of the 'Peplos Kore' in the Museum of Classical Archaeology in Cambridge. One of them is painted in bright reds, greens and blues as if its original colours were still preserved. (https://www.classics.cam.ac.uk/museum/collections/peplos-kore.)

Κόρινθος, Κορίνθου, ἡ **

noun

Corinth

....

κριτής, κριτοῦ, ὁ **

noun

judge

critic, critical, criticise, critique, diacritic,*[83] *literary criticism

....

κρύπτω, ἔκρυψα

verb

I hide (something)

***crypt, cryptaesthesia (cf. αἰσθάνομαι), cryptanalysis, cryptic, cryptogenic, cryptozoology*[84]**

....

κρύπτομαι, ἐκρυψάμην

verb

I hide (myself)

***see* κρύπτω**

....

---

[83] 'diacritic' is a sign, such as an accent, which is added above or below a letter to indicate e.g. a difference in pronunciation from when unmarked or differently marked.

[84] 'cryptozoology' is the study of and search for (potentially mythical) creatures, such as the Loch Ness monster.

κτάομαι, κτήσομαι, ἐκτησάμην

verb

I obtain, get

....

κωλύω, ἐκώλυσα *

verb

I hinder, prevent (someone from doing) (+ *accusative* + *infinitive*)

....

κώμη, κώμης, ἡ[85] **

noun

village

....

[85] A suggestion for remembering 'κωμη' is to transliterate it ('come') and to put it into a phrase such as 'Come to the village'. This may help avoid confusion with the similar word 'κορη'('girl') on which cf. the footnote to 'κορη', which may help with remembering its own meaning.

λ

λάθρᾳ

adverb

in secret, secretly

....

Λακεδαιμόνιοι, Λακεδαιμονίων, οἱ *

proper noun

the Spartans

....

λαμβάνω, λήψομαι, ἔλαβον, ἐλήφθην *

verb

I take, capture

analemma (cf. ἀνά), analeptic, -lepsy or -leptic (combining form signifying 'seizing' or 'seizure') e.g. catalepsy (cf. κατά), epilepsy (cf. ἐπί), proslambanomenos,[86] prolepsis,[87] syllable, syllepsis[88]

....

λέγω, ἐρῶ, (ἔλεξα *or)* εἶπον, ἐρρήθην *

verb

I say, speak, tell

dialect (cf. διά), lexicographer, lexicon, lexigram, lexis, prolegomena[89]

....

λείπω, λείψω, ἔλιπον, ἐλείφθην *

verb

I leave (behind)

ellipsis,[90] leipoa, lipogram

....

---

[86] In Greek music, the 'proslambanomenos' is an additional note at the bottom of the scale. It literally means 'being taken in addition'.

[87] 'prolepsis' is a form of anticipation in rhetoric, which can take various forms such as anticipating and addressing counter-arguments or objections.

[88] 'syllepsis' is when a word does what appears to be the same job in a sentence twice but each time it has a slightly different meaning, e.g.'she left in a huff and in a taxi' (based on an original idea from the 1933 film, *Duck Soup*).

[89] 'prolegomena' means an introduction.

[90] 'ellipsis' is the shortening of a sentence or phrase by the omission of words which can be undertood.

λίθος, λίθου, ὁ *

noun

stone

acrolith, epilithic (cf. ἐπί)

lith- or litho- (combining form signifying 'stone') e.g. lithochromy, lithoglyph, lithography, lithophagous (cf. ἐσθίω), lithophyte, lithoprint, lithotomy

....

λιμήν, λιμένος, ὁ *

noun

harbour

limen, liminal, liminality[91] (cf. 'limen' meaning 'threshold' in Latin)

....

[91] 'liminality' is a literary term which means the use of location, especially the threshold of a doorway, to symbolise a significant moment, e.g. Medea, in the eponymous play by Euripides, makes her dramatic entrance onto stage with the following words, 'Women of Corinth, I have come out of the house' and proceeds to deliver possibly her most powerful speech.

λόγος, λόγου, ὁ *

noun

word, speech, argument, story, account, reason
-logy (combining form signifying 'science' or 'theory')
e.g. biology, etymology, geology, theology
-logue (combining form signifying 'speech' or discourse')
e.g. dialogue (cf.* διά*), monologue (cf.* μόνος*)
apology, logarithm, logic, logogram, logomachy (cf.* μάχη*),
logophile, syllogism

....

λύω, ἔλυσα *

verb

I loose, untie, set free
analyse (cf.* ἀνά*), atmolysis,[92] ***hydrolysis***

....

[92] 'atmolysis' is a term in physics and chemistry.

μ

μάλιστα

superlative adverb

most, very much, especially

....

μᾶλλον

comparative adverb

more

....

μανθάνω, μαθήσομαι, ἔμαθον *

verb

I learn, understand

mathematics, mathematical, polymath

....

μάχη, μάχης, ἡ *

noun

battle, fight

gigantomachy, logomachy (cf. λόγος), promachos, theomachy (cf. θεός and corresponding footnote)

....

μάχομαι, μαχοῦμαι, ἐμαχεσάμην

verb

I fight

see μάχη

....

μέγας, μεγάλη, μέγα (μεγαλ-)

adjective

big, great

mega- (combining form signifying 'very big') e.g. megadose, megalithic, megalomania, megalopolis, megaphone

....

μέγιστος, μεγίστη, μέγιστον *

adjective

very great, very big

***see* μέγας**

....

μέλλω, μελλήσω, ἐμέλλησα + future infinitive

verb

I intend, am going to, hesitate

....

... μέν[93] ... δέ[94]*

particles

on the one hand… on the other [*marks a contrast*]

....

μέντοι[95] *

conjunction

however

....

μένω, μενῶ, ἔμεινα *

verb

I wait, remain

....

---

[93] Comes second word in sentence, clause or phrase.

[94] Comes second word in sentence, clause or phrase.

[95] Comes second word in sentence, clause or phrase.

μετά + acc *

preposition

after

meta- or met- (combining form signifying 'after', often implying change) e.g. metamorphosis, metaphysics, metonymy (cf. ὄνομα and corresponding footnote)

....

μετά + gen *

preposition

with

meta- or met- (combining form signifying 'with') e.g. metadata, metaphor (cf. φέρω)

....

μή[96]

adverb

not

....

μηδείς, μηδεμία, μηδέν (μηδεν-)

pronoun and adjective

no-one, nothing, no

....

[96] In general, 'μή' is used in expressing a negative opinion, wish or command, by contrast with 'οὐ', which is used to negate a fact or statement. The difference between the simple negatives holds true for their compounds. (*Cambridge Greek Lexicon* p931.)

μηδέποτε

adverb

never

....

μήτε … μήτε …

conjunctions

neither … nor …

....

μήτηρ, μητρός, ἡ

noun

mother

matriarch (cf. ἄρχων) (cf. 'mater' meaning 'mother' in Latin)

....

μικρός, μικρά, μικρόν *

adjective

little, small

micro- or micr- (combining form signifying 'very small') e.g. microblogging, microcapsule, microcephaly, microchip, microclimate, microfibre, microfilm, microphysics, micropolis, microscope, microsurgery, microwave, micrurgy (cf. ἔργον)

....

μισέω, ἐμίσησα

verb

I hate

misanthrope (cf. ἄνθρωπος), miso- (combining form signifying 'hating') e.g. misocapnic, misogamy, misogyny (cf. γυνή), misoneism (cf. νέος)

....

μόνος, μόνη, μόνον *

adjective

alone, only

mono- or mon- (combining form signifying 'alone' or 'single') e.g. monarch (cf. ἄρχων), monobrow, monochord, monochrome, monocle, monodrama, monogamy, monograph, monolith, monologue, monopod(e),[97] monopoly, monotone, monounsaturated, monoxide

....

---

[97] Pliny the Elder describes a race of people who are monopods (having one foot) who 'hop with amazing speed.' He continues, 'These people are also called the Umbrella-footed, because when the weather is hot they lie on their backs stretched out on the ground and protect themselves by the shade of their feet.' (Pliny, *Natural History* 7.2; translated by John F. Healy, Penguin Classics, 1991.)

μόνον *

adverb

only

see **μόνος**

....

μῦθος, μύθου, ὁ *

noun

story

myth, mythogenesis, mythographer, mythology, mythomania, mythopoetic (cf. **πoιέω*)***

....

μῶρος, μώρα, μῶρον *

adjective

foolish, stupid

moron, moronic, oxymoron[98]

....

[98] 'oxymoron' is a figure of speech by means of which contradictory terms are juxtaposed, for various effects, e.g. 'γλυκύπικρος' (literally, 'sweet-bitter' hence 'bitter-sweet') (Sappho, *Fragment* 130). In Greek 'oxymoron' means 'clever-stupid' and is an oxymoron itself.

ν

ναυμαχία, ναυμαχίας, ἡ **

noun

sea-battle

***see* ναῦς *and* μάχη**

....

ναῦς, νεώς, ἡ

noun

ship, warship

nautical, nautics, nautilus[99]

....

---

[99] A 'nautilus' is a cephalopod, i.e. a marine animal such as an octopus (cf. κεφαλή and corresponding footnote).

ναύτης, ναύτου, ὁ *

noun

sailor

***see* ναῦς**

....

ναυτικόν, ναυτικοῦ, τό *

noun

fleet

***see* ναῦς**

....

νεανίας, νεανίου, ὁ *

noun

young man

neanic

....

νεκρός, νεκροῦ, ὁ *

noun

corpse

necro- (combining form signifying 'dead' or 'dead body')
e.g. necrobiotic, necrology, necromancy, necrophagous, necrophorous, necropolis, necropsy, necrotomy

....

νέος, νέα, νέον *

adjective

new, young, recent

neo- (combining form signifying 'new') e.g. neoclassical, Neohellenism, neoblast,[100] neologism,[101] neon, neophile, neophobia, neoteric

....

νῆσος, νήσου, ἡ *

noun

island

....

[100] 'neoblast' is a term in zoology.

[101] 'neologisms' ('new words') were coined by Homer, probably for metrical purposes, and include compounds of 'μεγα-' and 'πολυ-'. (Stanford, vol. 2 pxix.)

νικάω, ἐνίκησα

verb

I win, conquer

***see* νίκη**

....

νίκη, νίκης, ἡ *

noun

victory

Nike (Athene's epithet as the Greek goddess of victory)

....

νομίζω, νομιῶ, ἐνόμισα

verb

I think, consider, believe

....

νόμος, νόμου, ὁ *

noun

law, custom

astronomy, autonomy, economy (cf.* οἰκέω*), nomo- (combining form signifying 'law' or 'custom') e.g. nomocracy, nomogeny, nomogram,*[102] *nomothete

....

[102] 'nomogram' and 'nomograph' are terms in mathematics.

νόσος, νόσου, ἡ *

noun

disease, illness

nosocomial, nosode, nosography, nosology, nosophobia

....

νῦν *

adverb

now

....

νύξ, νυκτός, ἡ *

noun

night

acronycal, noct- (combining form signifying 'night') e.g. noctambulist, nocturnal, nocturne (cf. 'nox' meaning 'night' in Latin)

....

ξ

ξένος, ξένου, ὁ *

noun

stranger, foreigner, host, guest, friend

xeno- or xen- (combining form signifying 'strange' or 'foreign' or 'guest') e.g. xenobiotic, xenogamy, xenomania, xenon,[103] xenophile, xenophobe, xenotransplant

....

[103] 'xenon' is a heavy, gaseous element (symbol Xe on the periodic table).

ξίφος, ξίφους, τό

noun

sword

Xiphias[104]

xiph- (combining form signifying 'sword')

e.g. xiphihumeralis, xiphoid, xiphophyllous[105]

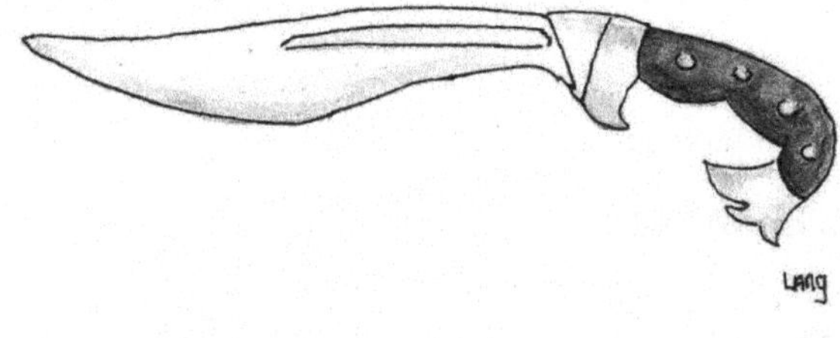

....

[104] Xiphias is the common swordfish genus (group).

[105] 'xiphophyllous' describes plants with sword-shaped leaves.

O

ὁ, ἡ, τό *

definite article

the

....

ὅδε, ἥδε, τόδε

demonstrative pronoun

this

....

ὁδός, ὁδοῦ, ἡ *

noun

road, path, way, journey

anode, cathode, electrode, hodoscope, hodograph, (h)odometer, (h)odometry, period, triode

....

οἶδα

verb

I know (*present, participle and infinitive only*)

……………………………………………………………

οἰκέω, ᾤκησα

verb

I live (in), inhabit, dwell

***dioecious,*[106] *ecology/oecology, economy (cf.* νόμος*), oecist/ oikist, trioecious*[107]**

……………………………………………………………

οἰκία, οἰκίας, ἡ *

noun

house, home

***see* οἰκέω**

……………………………………………………………

οἶνος, οἴνου, ὁ *

noun

wine

oino-, oeno- or oen- (combining form signifying 'wine) e.g. oenanthic, oenology, oenomancy, oenomel, oenometer, oenophile

……………………………………………………………

---

106 'dioecious' is a term in biology.

107 'trioecious' is a botanical term.

οἷός τ᾽ εἰμί *

adjectival phrase

I am able, can

....

ὀκτώ *

cardinal number

eight

oct-, octa- or octo- (combining form signifying 'eight') e.g. octocentenary, octogenarian, octohedron, octopetalous, octopus (cf. πούς), octosyllabic, octuplet

....

ὀλίγος, ὀλίγη, ὀλίγον *

adjective

little

olig- or oligo- (combining form signifying 'little' or 'few') e.g. oligaemia, oligarch, oligochrome, oligopoly, oligotrophic, oliguria[108]

....

ὀλίγοι, ὀλίγαι, ὀλίγα *

adjective

few

***see* ὀλίγος**

....

---

108 'oliguria' is a medical term.

ὄνομα, ὀνόματος, τό *

noun

name

***acronym, allonym, anonymous, antonomasia, antonym, eponymous, homonym, hypernym, metonymy*[109] *(cf.* μετά*), onomastic, onomatopoeia,*[110] *paronomasia,*[111] *patronymic,*[112] *polyonymous, synonym, teknonymy, trionym*[113]**

....

ὅπλα, ὅπλων, τά *

noun

weapons, arms, armour

hoplite, hoplology, hoplologist

....

---

[109] 'metonymy' is a way of describing persons or objects by something with which they are associated. Greek poets often use the names of gods to denote their associated attribute, e.g. Dionysus, also known by his title 'Bacchus', can mean 'wine'.

[110] A lovely example of 'onomatopoeia' (where the sounds of words suggest their sense) recurs in Aristophanes' *Frogs* (e.g. 209–10): 'βρεκεκεκὲξ κοὰξ κοάξ' describing the croaking of frogs.

[111] 'paronomasia' is a pun, e.g. the play on the words 'Οὖτις, μή τίς' and 'μῆτις' in Homer's *Odyssey* 9.364ff. where Odysseus tells Polyphemus his name is 'Nobody' leading Polyphemus to say 'Nobody is hurting me' when his fellow Cyclopes come to help. The pun includes 'μῆτις' meaning 'trickery', a hallmark of Odysseus.

[112] Patronymics are used in Homer to describe the main characters by reference to their father, e.g. 'Ἀτρεΐδης' ('Son of Atreus') for Agamemnon and Menelaus, or 'Λαερτιάδης' ('Son of Laertes') for Odysseus. They are rarer in the *Odyssey* than in the *Iliad*. Curiously, Telemachus is never given one. (Stanford, vol. 2 p232.)

[113] 'trionym' (or a 'trinomial') is a term in biology meaning 'consisting of three terms' (for genus, species and subspecies) and is also a term in mathematics meaning 'consisting of three terms connected by the plus or minus sign'.

ὁράω, ὄψομαι, εἶδον, ὤφθην

verb

I see

optic, optical, ophthalm- (combining form signifying 'eye') e.g. ophthalmology, ophthalmometer, ophthalmophobia, ophthalmoscope, synopsis

....

ὀργίζομαι, ὀργιοῦμαι, ὠργίσθην + dat

verb

I grow angry (with)

....

ὄρος, ὄρους, τό

noun

mountain, hill

orogenesis, orography, orology

....

ὅς, ἥ, ὅ

relative pronoun
who, which

....

ὅτι

conjunction
that

....

οὐ, οὐκ (before smooth breathing), οὐχ (before rough breathing)[114] *

adverb
not

....

οὐδείς, οὐδεμία, οὐδέν (οὐδεν-) *

pronoun and adjective
no-one, nothing, no

....

οὐδέποτε

adverb
never

....

[114] In general, 'οὐ' is used to negate a fact or statement, by contrast with 'μή', which is used in expressing a negative opinion, wish or command. The difference between the simple negatives holds true for their compounds. (*Cambridge Greek Lexicon* p1035.)

οὔτε … οὔτε

conjunctions

neither … nor …

……………………………………………………………

οὖν[115] *

particle

therefore, and so

……………………………………………………………

οὐρανός, οὐρανοῦ, ὁ

noun

sky, heaven

Urania,*[116] *Uranus,*[117] *uranic, uranium, urano- (combining form denoting 'sky' or 'heaven') e.g. uranographer, uranology, uranometry

……………………………………………………………

[115] Comes second word in sentence, clause or phrase.

[116] In Greek mythology Urania was the Muse of astronomy. Urania is also an epithet of Aphrodite.

[117] 'Uranus/Ouranos' or 'Heaven' is the father of Kronos, whose mother is 'Ge' (cf. γῆ) or 'Earth'. 'Uranus' is also the name given to a planet discovered in 1781.

οὗτος, αὕτη, τοῦτο

demonstrative pronoun

this

....

οὕτω(ς)

adverb

so, in this way

....

π

παῖς, παιδός, ὁ and ἡ *

noun

child, son, daughter, boy, girl

paed-, ped- or paid- (combining form signifying 'child')
e.g. paediatric (cf. ἰατρός), paedodontics, paedology, pedagogue (cf. ἄγω), propaedeutic

....

πάλαι *

adverb

long ago, in the past, formerly

palae- or palaeo- (combining form signifying 'old' or 'concerning the distant past')
e.g. palaeanthropic, palaebiology, palaeobotany, Palaeolithic, palaeopedology, palaeotype, palaeozoology

....

παρά + acc

preposition

contrary to, along, to

para- (prefix meaning 'beside' or 'parallel to') e.g. paramedic, paramilitary, parabasis (cf. βαίνω and corresponding footnote), parable (cf. βάλλω), paragraph, paralegal, parallel, parallelogram, paralympics, paralysis (cf. λύω), paraphernalia (cf. φέρω), paraphrase, parasite, parenthesis, parody

para- (prefix meaning 'contrary to') e.g. paradox (cf. δοκεῖ)

....

παρά + gen

preposition

from (a person)

....

παρασκευάζω, παρεσκεύασα *

verb

I prepare

skeuomorph, skeuomorphic

....

πάρειμι, *imperfect* παρῆν *

verb

I am here, I am present

....

παρέχω, παρέσχον *

verb

I provide, cause, produce

....

πᾶς, πᾶσα, πᾶν (παντ-) *

adjective

all, every

pan-, pant- or panto (combining form signifying 'all') e.g. panacea, pandemic (cf. δῆμος), panegyric, pangram, panhellenic, panoptic, panorama, pansophy, pantomime, pantheon

....

πάσχω, πείσομαι, ἔπαθον *

verb

I suffer, experience

(various combining forms signifying 'suffering', 'experience' or 'healing/treatment') e.g. antipathy, apathy, empathy, homeopathy (cf. ἄλλος), osteopath, pathogen, pathology, pathos, pathetic fallacy, psychopath, sympathy

....

πατήρ, πατρός, ὁ

noun

father

patriarch (cf. ἄρχων), patriarchy

....

παύω, ἔπαυσα *

verb

I stop

menopause, pausal, pause

....

παύομαι, ἐπαυσάμην (middle)

verb

I stop, cease from (doing something)

see παύω

....

πείθω, ἔπεισα *

verb

I persuade

....

πείθομαι, πείσομαι, ἐπιθόμην + dat

verb

I obey

....

πειράομαι, πειράσομαι

verb

I try

peirastic, peirastically

....

πέμπτος, πέμπτη, πέμπτον *

ordinal number

fifth

....

πέμπω, ἔπεμψα *

verb

I send, escort

apopemptic,[118] ***hypnopompic (cf. ὕπνος), pomp, pomposity, pompous***

....

[118] 'apopemptic' is a rare word meaning 'valedictory' (cf. 'vale' meaning 'goodbye' or 'farewell' in Latin), literally 'sending away'.

πέντε *

cardinal number

five

pent- or penta- (combining form signifying 'five') e.g. pentachord, pentadactyl, pentagon, pentagram, pentahedron, pentalogy, pentameter,[119] pentastyle (cf. δέκα and corresponding footnote), pentathlon, pentoxide

....

περί + acc

preposition

round

peri- (combining form signifying 'round') e.g. peribolos (cf. βάλλω), perigee[120] (cf. γῆ), perimeter, period (cf. ὁδός), periodical, peripatetic, peripeteia (cf. πίπτω), periphery (cf. φέρω), periphrasis[121]

....

περί + gen *

preposition

about, concerning

....

---

[119] A 'pentameter' is a line of verse of five measures or 'feet'. Emily Wilson's recent English translations of Homer's *Iliad* (W.W. Norton & Company, 2023) and *Odyssey* (W.W. Norton & Company, 2017) are in iambic pentameters, a metre used in much English verse including Shakespeare's plays. (See further: Taylor, *Greek Beyond GCSE* p205.)

[120] 'perigee' is a term in astronomy.

[121] 'periphrasis' means a roundabout way of saying something, or using more words than necessary, e.g. 'νόστιμον ἦμαρ' ('day of returning') instead of 'νόστος' ('return'). (Homer, *Odyssey* 19.369.)

Πέρσαι, Περσῶν, οἱ **

noun

the Persians

....

πίνω, πιοῦμαι, ἔπιον *

verb

I drink

symposium[122]

....

πίπτω, πεσοῦμαι, ἔπεσον *

verb

I fall

asymptote,[123] ***peripeteia, ptosis, tetraptote***[124] ***(cf. τέσσαρες), triptote***[125] ***(cf. τρεῖς)***

....

---

[122] A 'symposium' is a drinking party in ancient Greece. Plato's *Symposium*, written in the early part of the fourth century BC, is set at a drinking party at which the guests are some of the pre-eminent intellectuals of the day. The cover image of this lexicon depicts the interior of a 'kylix' ('drinking bowl') which would have been used at a symposium. (https://id.smb.museum/object/686555/attische-trinkschale-im-frauengemach.)

[123] 'asymptote' is a term in mathematics meaning a line that continually approaches a curve but never meets it.

[124] 'tetraptote' means a word with only four cases. The term 'case' derives from the Latin 'casus' ('a fall'): the various other cases 'fall away' from the nominative as the noun declines. (Cullen and Taylor, *Latin to GCSE 1* p11, Bloomsbury 2016.)

[125] 'triptote' means a word with only three cases. See footnote on 'tetraptote' for the origin of the word 'case'.

πιστεύω, ἐπίστευσα + dat *

verb

I trust, believe

....

πιστός, πιστή, πιστόν

adjective

faithful, reliable

....

πλέω, πλεύσομαι, ἔπλευσα

verb

I sail

....

πλήν

conjunction

except

....

πλοῖον, πλοίου, τό[126] *

noun

boat, cargo ship

....

πλούσιος, πλουσία, πλούσιον

adjective

rich

pluto- (combining form signifying 'wealth') e.g. plutocrat, plutodemocracy, plutolatry, plutology, plutonomy

....

ποιέω, ἐποίησα

verb

I do, make

mythopoetic (cf. μῦθος), poem, poet, poetic, poetry

....

---

126 A possible way to remember 'πλοῖον' is that it rhymes with 'buoy', something that is associated with boats.

ποιητής, ποιητοῦ, ὁ **

noun
poet
see ποιέω

....

ποῖος, ποία, ποῖον;

interrogative adjective
what sort of?

....

πόλεμος, πολέμου, ὁ *

noun
war
polemarch, polemic, polemist

....

πολέμιοι, πολεμίων, οἱ *

noun
enemy (in war) (cf. **ἐχθρός**)
see πόλεμος

....

πόλις, πόλεως, ἡ

noun
city, state
acropolis, police, policy, political, politics

....

πολίτης, πολίτου, ὁ *

noun

citizen

***see* πόλις**

....

πολλάκις *

adverb

often

....

πολύς, πολλή, πολύ (πολλ-)[127]

adjective

much

poly- (combining form signifying 'much' or 'many') e.g. polyanthus, polyarch, polyester, polygamous, polyglot, polymath, Polyphemus,[128] polystyrene, polysyllabic, polysyndeton,[129] polytunnel, polyunsaturated

....

---

[127] The comparative of 'πολύς' is 'πλείων' ('more') which gives us words such as 'pleonasm', a literary term meaning use of more words than are necessary to convey meaning.

[128] Polyphemus is one of the Cyclopes and the son of Poseidon; his encounter with Odysseus is recounted by Homer in *Odyssey* 9. Polyphemus is also one of the characters in Euripides' *Cyclops* (*c.* 408 BC), which is the only complete surviving example of a satyr play. In Ovid's *Metamorphoses* 13, Polyphemus is the rejected lover of the nymph Galatea. Turner's 1829 painting *Ulysses Deriding Polyphemus* is on display at the National Gallery in London. (https://www.nationalgallery.org.uk/paintings/joseph-mallord-william-turner-ulysses-deriding-polyphemus-homer-s-odyssey.)

[129] 'polysyndeton' is a literary device whereby connectives or conjunctions are deliberately repeated.

πολλοί, πολλαί, πολλά *

adjective

many

***see* πολύς**

....

πορεύομαι, πορεύσομαι, ἐπορεύθην

verb

I travel, march

....

πόσος, πόση, πόσον;

interrogative adjective

how big? how much?

....

πόσοι, πόσαι, πόσα;

interrogative adjective

how many?

....

ποταμός, ποταμοῦ, ὁ *

noun

river

hippopotamus (cf.* ἵππος*), potamic, potamogeton, potamology

....

πότε; *

interrogative adverb

when?

....

ποῦ; *

interrogative adverb

where?

....

ποῖ;

interrogative adverb

to where?

....

πόθεν; *

interrogative adverb

from where?

....

πούς, ποδός, ὁ *

noun

foot

pod-, podo- or -pod (combining form signifying 'foot') e.g. antipodes, cephalopod (cf. κεφαλή and corresponding footnote), chiropodist (cf. χείρ), decapod,[130] podiatry (cf. ἰατρός), podophthalmous,[131] tripod[132]

....

[130] A 'decapod' is a member of the order of higher crustaceans with ten feet (including pincers), i.e. crabs, lobsters, shrimps, prawns, etc.

[131] 'podophthalmous' means having eyes on stalks, as do many higher crustaceans.

[132] Tripods ('three-legged' stands, sometimes with cauldrons attached, for cooking over a fire) are frequently mentioned in Homer as gifts or prizes in contests, e.g. *Iliad* 8.290, 11.700, 23.264,702.

πράσσω, πράξω, ἔπραξα, ἐπράχθην

verb

I do, fare, manage

apraxia, chiropractor (cf.* χείρ*), dyspraxia, practical, practice, pragmatic, praxis, Praxiteles[133]

....

πρό + gen

preposition

before, in front of

pro- (combining form signifying 'before') e.g. probouleutic (cf.* βουλή*), proceleusmatic (cf.* κελεύω*), prolegomena (cf.* λέγω *and corresponding footnote), prolepsis (cf.* λαμβάνω *and corresponding footnote), prologue, promachos, pronoun, prognosis (cf.* γιγνώσκω*), prophylactic (cf.* φύλαξ*), protasis[134] [135]

....

---

[133] Praxiteles was an Athenian sculptor of the mid-fourth century BC. One of his most celebrated statues was his 'Aphrodite of Knidos'. Upon seeing it, Aphrodite herself was said to have remarked, 'Where did Praxiteles see me naked?' (*Greek Anthology* 6.160.) Pliny the Elder tells the following anecdote: 'There is a story that a man who had fallen in love with the statue hid in the temple at night and embraced it intimately; a stain bears witness to his lust.' (*Natural History* 36.4; translated by John F. Healy, Penguin Classics, 1991.)

[134] The 'protasis' is the 'if' half of a conditional sentence, (i.e. not the half expressing the consequence, which is the 'apodosis'). 'Protasis' literally means 'put forward' as a premise. The 'protasis' usually comes before the 'apodosis' but (in both Greek and English) can come after it. (Taylor, *Greek to GCSE 2* p188.)

[135] The 'protasis' is also the initial part of a drama as opposed to the 'epitasis' which is the main action of a Greek drama building up to the catastrophe.

πρός + acc *

preposition

to, towards, against

proslambanomenos (cf. λαμβάνω and corresponding footnote), prosody

....

προσάγω, προσήγαγον *

verb

I lead to(wards)

***see* ἄγω**

....

προσβαίνω, προσέβην * (Aorist tense not needed for the ICCG)

verb

I go towards

***see* βαίνω**

....

προσβάλλω, προσέβαλον + dat

verb

I attack

***see* βάλλω**

....

προσπέμπω, προσέπεμψα *

verb

I send to(wards)

***see* πέμπω**

....

προστρέχω, προσέδραμον *

verb

I run towards

***see* τρέχω**

....

πρότερον *

adverb

before, formerly

***proterandry,*[136] *proterogyny (cf.* γυνή*), Proterozoic, hysteron proteron*[137]**

....

πρῶτος, πρώτη, πρῶτον *

ordinal number

first

proto- or prot- (combining form signifying 'first') e.g. protagonist, protein, protocol, proto-history, proton, prototype

....

πρῶτον *

adverb

at first, first

....

---

[136] 'proterandry' is a term in both zoology and botany.

[137] 'hysteron proteron' is a literary device whereby the normal (temporal) order of events is reversed, e.g. 'εἵματά τ' ἀμφιέσασα θυώδεα καὶ λούσασα', 'having dressed [Odysseus] in fragrant clothes and washed him'. (Homer, *Odyssey* 5.264.)

πύλη, πύλης, ἡ *

noun

gate

Propylaia,[138] ***pylon, pylorus***[139]

....

πυνθάνομαι, πεύσομαι, ἐπυθόμην

verb

I learn, ascertain, ask

....

138 The 'Propylaia' is the monumental entrance, or gateway, to the Acropolis in Athens, built 437–432 BC.

139 The 'pylorus' is the opening, or gateway, from the stomach to the intestines.

πῦρ, πυρός, τό *

noun

fire

antipyretic, pyral, pyre, pyretology, pyretotherapy, pyrexia, pyrheliometer, pyro- (combining form signifying 'fire') e.g. pyroballogy (cf. βάλλω), pyrogenic, pyromaniac, pyrotechnics

....

πῶς; *

interrogative adverb

how?

....

ῥ

ῥᾴδιος, ῥᾳδία, ῥᾴδιον

adjective

easy

....

σ

σιγή, σιγῆς, ἡ

noun

silence

....

σῖτος, σίτου, ὁ

noun

food, corn, bread

sitology, sitophobia

....

σοφία, σοφίας, ἡ **

noun

wisdom

Sophia, Sophie; see σοφός

....

σοφός, σοφή, σοφόν *

adjective

wise, clever

philosophy, sophism, sophisticated, sophomore

....

στρατηγοῦ, ὁ *

noun

general, commander

stratagem, strategy, strategic

....

στρατιά, στρατιᾶς, ἡ

noun

army

stratocracy, stratocrat

....

στρατιώτης, στρατιώτου, ὁ *

noun

soldier

***see* στρατιά**

στρατόπεδον, στρατοπέδου, το **

noun

camp

***see* στρατός *and* πούς**

στρατός, στρατοῦ, ὁ **

noun

army

stratocracy, stratocrat

....

σύ, σοῦ *

pronoun

you

....

σός, σή, σόν *

possessive adjective

your

....

συλλέγω, συλλέξω, συνέλεξα *

verb

I collect, assemble

....

σύμμαχοι, συμμάχων, οἱ *

noun

allies

***see* μάχη**

....

συμφορά, συμφορᾶς, ἡ

noun

misfortune, disaster, event

....

σῴζω, σώσω, ἔσωσα, ἐσώθην

verb

I save, keep, get away safely (*passive*)

soterial, soteriology

....

σῶμα, σώματος, τό *

noun

body

soma, somascope, somatism, somatosensory, somatotype

....

τ

τάσσω, ἔταξα **

verb

I draw up, arrange

***syntax, taxidermy, taxis,*[140] *taxonomy*[141]**

....

ταχύς, ταχεῖα, ταχύ[142]

adjective

fast, quick

tacho- or tachy- (combining form signifying 'fast')
***e.g. tachograph, tachometer, tachycardia, tachygrapher, tachypnea, tachyon*[143]**
***see* ὡς τάχιστα**

....

[140] A 'taxis' is a division of an ancient Greek army. It is a term in medicine, particularly surgery.

[141] 'taxonomy' is a classification (particularly of plants or animals) or its principles.

[142] A 'tachistoscope' derives from the superlative form of 'ταχύς', which is 'τάχιστος' ('quickest', 'very quick'). A 'tachistoscope' is a piece of equipment that projects images, sentences, etc. onto a screen at controlled speed, used e.g. to test speed of comprehension, and also to increase reading speed.

[143] 'tachyon' is a term in physics.

... τε[144] ... καί *

conjunctions

both … and

…………………………………………………………………

τεῖχος, τείχους, τό

noun

wall

teichopsia

…………………………………………………………………

τέλος *

adverb

end (adv. in the end), at last, finally

telic, telocentric, telomere, telophase, telos

…………………………………………………………………

144 Comes second word in sentence, clause or phrase.

τέσσαρες, τέσσαρες, τέσσαρα *

cardinal number

four

tessera,*[145] *tessara- or tessera- (combining form signifying 'four') e.g. tessaraglot, tesseract

tetra- or tetr- (combining form signifying 'four') e.g. tetrachord,*[146] *tetradactyl, tetradrachm,*[147] *tetragon, tetragram, tetrahedron, tetrapod, tetraptote (cf. πίπτω and corresponding footnote), tetrarch, tetrastyle (cf. δέκα and corresponding footnote), tetrasyllabic, tetrathlon

....

τέταρτος, τετάρτη, τέταρτον *

ordinal number

fourth

tetartohedral

....

τιμάω, ἐτίμησα

verb

I honour, respect

timocracy

....

[145] A 'tessera' is a small cube-shaped piece of stone, glass or other material from which a mosaic is made. Mosaics from Roman Britain often depict scenes from Greek mythology, e.g. Bellerophon fighting the Chimaera. (See further: *Culture and Society at Lullingstone Roman Villa*, Caroline K. Mackenzie (Archaeopress, 2019).)

[146] In Greek music, a 'tetrachord' is a series of tones and semitones spanning the interval of a fourth.

[147] A 'tetradrachm' is an ancient Greek coin worth four drachmas.

τίμη, τιμῆς, ἡ *

noun

honour

***see* τιμάω**

....

τις, τι (τιν-)[148] *

indefinite adjective/pronoun

(a) certain, someone, something

***see footnote on 'enclitic' under* ἐν**

....

τίς; τί; (τίν-)[149] *

interrogative adjective/pronoun

who? what? which?

....

τοιοῦτος, τοιαύτη, τοιοῦτο

demonstrative adjective

such

....

---

[148] Never as first word in a sentence or clause, and when used as an adjective must follow its noun. See also Taylor, *Greek to GCSE 1* pp98–9 on the uses of τίς/τις and the notes there on accents.

[149] Usually comes first in its clause. See also Taylor, *Greek to GCSE 1* pp98–9 on the uses of τίς/τις and the notes there on accents.

τόπος, τόπου, ὁ *

noun

place

topography, topology, toponym (cf.* ὄνομα*),
topophilia, topotype

....

τοσοῦτος, τοσαύτη, τοσοῦτο

demonstrative adjective

so great

....

τοσοῦτοι, τοσαῦται, τοσαῦτα

demonstrative adjective

so many

....

τότε

adverb

then, at that time

....

τρεῖς, τρεῖς, τρία *

cardinal number

three

tri- (combining form signifying 'three') e.g. triakisoctahedron,[150] triangle, triapsidal, triathlon, tribrach, tricephalous, triceps, trident, triglyph,[151] trigonometry, trigonon,[152] trigram, trilogy, tripod (cf. πούς and corresponding footnote), triptote (cf. πίπτω and corresponding footnote), trisoctahedron[153]

....

τρέχω, δραμοῦμαι, ἔδραμον *

verb

I run

anadromous (cf. ἀνά), dromophobia, dromos, hippodrome

....

τρίτος, τρίτη, τρίτον *

ordinal number

third

tritagonist,[154] tritanopia, tritium;[155]
see τρεῖς

....

---

[150] A 'triakisoctahedron' is a solid figure like an octahedron with a three-faced pyramid on each face.

[151] A 'triglyph' is a three-grooved tablet in the frieze of a Doric temple, such as the Parthenon. Between the triglyphs are square spaces called metopes, which often illustrate episodes from Greek mythology. (https://www.britishmuseum.org/collection/galleries/greece-parthenon.)

[152] A 'trigonon' is an ancient Greek triangle or a triangular harp.

[153] A 'trisoctahedron' is another name for 'triakisoctahedron' (see above).

[154] A 'tritagonist' is the third actor in a Greek play.

[155] 'tritium' is a term in chemistry.

τύχη, τύχης, ἡ

noun

chance, luck, fortune (good or bad)

Tyche*,**[156] ***tychism

....

[156] Tyche is the Greek goddess of fortune.

υ

ὕδωρ, ὕδατος, τό *

noun

water

anhydride, hydro- or hydr- (combining form signifying 'water') e.g. dehydrate, hydrangea, hydrate, hydraulic, hydria,[157] hydrocephalus (cf. κεφαλή), hydroelectric, hydrogen, hydrolysis

....

υἱός, υἱοῦ, ὁ

noun

son

....

---

157 A 'hydria' is the name of a vase or jar used in ancient Greece for fetching water. Often these vases were highly decorated with scenes from mythology. A hydria in the Museum of Fine Arts, Boston depicts the chariot of Achilles dragging the corpse of Hektor (520–510 BC). (https://collections.mfa.org/objects/153447/water-jar-hydria-with-the-chariot-of-achilles-dragging-the.)

ὕλη, ὕλης, ἡ

noun

wood, forest

hyle, hylic, hylogenesis, hylomorphic, hylopathism (cf. πάσχω), hylotheism

....

ὑμεῖς, ὑμῶν *

pronoun

you (plural)

....

ὑμέτερος, ὑμετέρα, ὑμέτερον *

possessive adjective

your

....

ὑπέρ + gen

preposition
on behalf of

....

ὑπισχνέομαι, ὑποσχήσομαι, ὑπεσχόμην

verb
I promise

....

ὕπνος, ὕπνου, ὁ *

noun
sleep
hypno- or hypn- (combining form signifying 'sleep')
e.g. hypnogogic, hypnopompic (cf. πέμπω), Hypnos,[158]
hypnotherapy, hypnotise

....

ὑπό + gen

preposition
by (*with the agent of passive verbs*)

....

[158] Hypnos is the Greek god of sleep.

ὕστερον

adverb

later

hysteron proteron (cf.* πρότερον *and corresponding footnote)

....

ὑψηλός, ὑψηλή, ὑψηλόν

adjective

high

hypso- (combining form signifying 'height') e.g. hypsography, hypsometer, hypsophobia

....

φαίνομαι, φανοῦμαι, ἐφάνην

verb

I seem, appear

angelophany, fantasy, hierophant, phantom, phenomenon, phenotype, sycophant, theophany

....

φέρω, οἴσω, ἤνεγκα, ἠνέχθην *

verb

I carry, bear, endure

-phore or -phor (combining form signifying 'carrier' or 'bearing') e.g. amphora,[159] anaphora,[160] chromatophore,[161] feretory, moschophoros,[162] paraphernalia (cf. παρά), pheromone, semaphore

....

φεύγω, φεύξομαι, ἔφυγον *

verb

I run away, flee, am accused, am banished

apophyge,[163] fugitive, refuge (cf. 'fugio' meaning 'I flee' in Latin)

....

---

[159] An 'amphora' is a two-handled Greek vase, from 'φέρω' ('I carry') and 'ἀμφί' ('on both sides'). An amphora (*c.* 520 BC) in the Metropolitan Museum in New York depicts Heracles bringing the Erymanthian Boar to King Eurystheus, and on the other side it depicts Ajax carrying the body of Achilles. (https://www.metmuseum.org/art/collection/search/254878.)

[160] 'anaphora' is the repetition of a word or phrase in successive sentences or clauses, e.g. 'οἴκαδε ἱέμενοι ἄλλην ὁδὸν, ἄλλα κέλευθα, | ἤλθομεν' ('journeying home we have come another way, on other paths'). (Homer, *Odyssey* 9.261-2.)

[161] 'chromatophore' is a term in biology.

[162] The 'moschophoros' (literally meaning 'calf-bearer') is the name of a marble statue dating to *c.* 570 BC and found on the Acropolis in Athens in 1864 during construction works for the old Acropolis Museum. It is now housed in the Acropolis Museum in Athens. (https://www.theacropolismuseum.gr/en/male-statue-its-base-calf-bearer.) There is also a cast of the statue in the Museum of Classical Archaeology in Cambridge. (https://museum.classics.cam.ac.uk/collections/casts/moschophoros.)

[163] 'apophyge' is a term in architecture to describe the curve where a column meets its base or capital.

φημί, φήσω, ἔφην

verb

I say

aphasia, dysphasia, euphemism (cf.* εὖ *and corresponding footnote), phasis

....

φιλέω, ἐφίλησα

verb

I love, like, am accustomed

phil- or philo- (combining form signifying 'lover of' or 'loving') e.g. philanthropy, philharmonic, philhellenic, philology, philomath, philosopher

-phil or -phile (suffix meaning 'lover of' or 'loving') bibliophile, Hellenophile, linguaphile, logophile, oenophile

-philus (suffix in biological names meaning 'lover of', usually a specified food)

....

φίλη, φίλης, ἡ

noun

(female) friend

***see* φιλέω**

....

φίλος, φίλου, ὁ *

noun

(male) friend

***see* φιλέω**

....

φοβέομαι, φοβήσομαι, ἐφοβήθην

verb

I am afraid, fear

phobia, phobic

-phobe (combining form signifying someone who has a specified fear or hatred) e.g. hypsophobe, xenophobe

-phobia (combining form signifying a fear or hatred of a specified object or condition) e.g. arachnophobia, triskaidekaphobia

....

φόβος, φόβου, ὁ *

noun

fear

***see* φοβέομαι**

....

φονεύω, ἐφόνευσα

verb

I murder, kill

....

φύλαξ, φύλακος, ὁ *

noun

guard

***see* φυλάσσω**

....

φυλάσσω, ἐφύλαξα *

verb

I guard

anaphylactic, phylactery, prophylactic (cf. πρό)

....

φωνή, φωνῆς, ἡ *

noun

voice

aphonia, euphony (cf. εὖ),[164] ***symphony***

-phone (combining form signifying 'speaking' or 'sound')

e.g. Francophone, megaphone, microphone, telephone

phono- (combining form signifying 'voice' or 'sound')

e.g. phonocardiogram, phonogram, phonophobia, phonophore

....

[164] 'euphony' means the beautiful sound of words, e.g. 'πὰρ ποταμὸν κελάδοντα, παρὰ ῥοδανὸν δονακῆα' ('by a flowing river, by swaying reeds'). (Homer, *Iliad* 18.576.) (See discussion in Stanford, vol. 2 pxxii.)

χ

χαλεπός, χαλεπή, χαλεπόν[165] *

adjective

difficult, dangerous, harsh

....

χειμών, χειμῶνος, ὁ

noun

storm, winter

Chimonanthus[166]

....

---

165 A suggestion for remembering 'χαλεπός' is to transliterate the first three letters to 'chal' which are the first letters in the word 'challenge'.

166 'Chimonanthus' is a deciduous genus (group) of shrubs native to China including the species 'winter-sweet', known for its yellow spicy-scented flowers, which appear in winter.

χείρ, χειρός, ἡ

noun

hand

***chiro- or cheiro- (combining form signifying 'hand') e.g. chirognomy, chirograph, chironomy, chiropractor (cf. πράσσω), chiropodist (cf. πούς), chiropteran,*[167] *chiropterophilous*[168]**

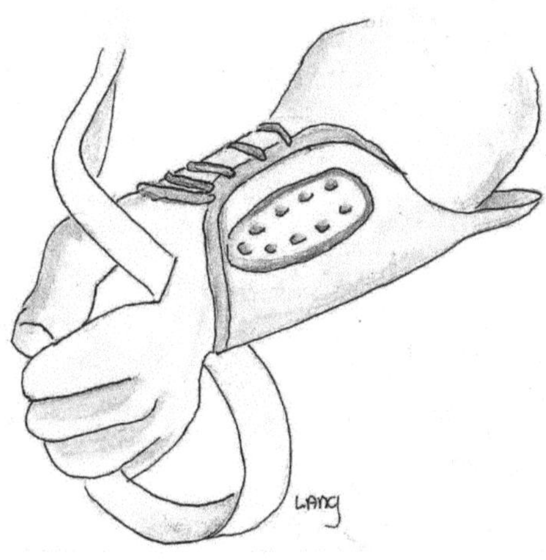

....

[167] A 'chiropteran' is a member of the Chiroptera, an order of mammals comprising bats.

[168] 'chiropterophilous' describes flowers which are pollinated by bats.

χράομαι, χρήσομαι, ἐχρησάμην + dat

verb

I use, treat

....

χρή with acc + infinitive

impersonal verb

it is necessary

....

χρήματα, χρημάτων, τά *

noun

money, goods, property

chrematist, chrematistics

....

χρήσιμος, χρησίμη, χρήσιμον *

adjective

useful

chrestomathy[169] ***(cf. μανθάνω), chrestomathic***

....

[169] A 'chrestomathy' is an anthology of literary passages, usually for students of a foreign language.

χρόνος, χρόνου, ὁ *

noun

time

chron- or chrono- (combining form signifying 'time') e.g. anachronistic (cf. ἀνά), chronic, chronicle, 'chronique scandaleuse',[170] chronobiology, chronogram,[171] chronology, chronometer, synchronise

....

χρυσός, χρυσοῦ, ὁ

noun

gold

chrys- or chryso- (combining form signifying 'gold'), e.g. chrysalis, chrysanthemum, chryselephantine,[172] chrysocracy, chrysophilite

....

χώρα, χώρας, ἡ *

noun

country, land

chorepiscopal, chorography, chorology, choropleth map[173]

....

---

170 A 'chronique scandaleuse' is a story or gossip full of scandal, or unsavoury 'tittle-tattle'.

171 A 'chronogram' is an inscription or phrase in which letters form a date in Roman numerals.

172 Pheidias' colossal statue of Athena Parthenos (447–438 BC) in her temple, the Parthenon, on the Acropolis in Athens was chryselephantine (gold and ivory). It is described by Pausanias in his *Description of Greece* 1.24.5–7.

173 A 'choropleth map' is a map in which areas of land that have similar geography or, say, climate are shown in a corresponding colour.

ω

ὦ *

interjection

o … (addressing someone)

....

ὥρα, ὥρας, ἡ **

noun

hour

Horae,*[174] *horography, horologe, horometry, horoscope

....

174 The 'Horae' were the Greek goddesses of the hours.

ὡς *

conjunction

when, as, because

(+ *present or past participle*) as, since, because, on the grounds that

(+ *future participle*) in order to

....

ὡς τάχιστα

adverbial phrase

as quickly (or other superlative) as possible

see ταχύς and corresponding footnote

....

ὥστε

conjunction

that, so that, with the result that

....